Beginner
+
Intermediate
Guide to Celtic Patterns

© Copyright 2019 - All rights reserved.

It is not legal to reproduce, duplicate, or transmit any part of this document in either electronic means or in printed format. Recording of this publication is strictly prohibited and any storage of this document is not allowed unless with written permission from the publisher except for the use of brief quotations in a book review.

Table of Contents

Celtic Patterns for Beginners

Abby O'Shea

Introduction

Humans' love and admiration for aesthetics permeate back hundreds of thousands of years. Humans across the world have created objects to symbolize their cultures, beliefs, interests, and other life areas, just for pleasure. What they did then was just for fun. Little did they know that they were laying the foundation for the birth of art. During the Middle Ages, Celtic Art, often considered as the ancient inhabitants of Britain and Ireland, was born. It was believed that Celtic art was practiced as early as the 5th century. Celts' art, also known as Celtic art, focused mainly on ornamental artistry made up of patterns, knots, foliage, spirals, and animals. These ornamental designs were mainly symbols of natural elements such as water, air, fire, and other spiritual entities. Celts were busy migrating from one place to the other because of the ongoing wars of the Iron Age. So, they learned so many things about the cultures of the places they visited and incorporated those cultures in their art.

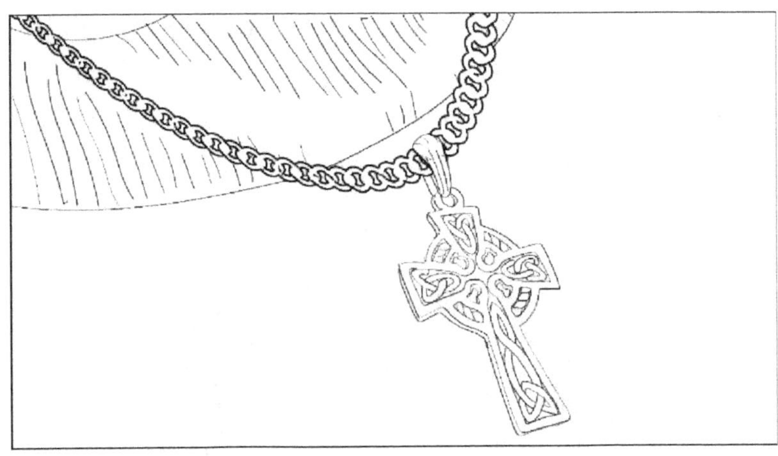

The constant wars of the period aided the spread of Celtic art across distant lands. Celts migrated and changed locations at the time, and other people had access to their rich cultural heritage. Celts' belief in superstition was second to none at the time. And, since it was a period people had so much respect and reverence for superstition and religion, everyone was eager to learn the Celts' way of life. So, just before anyone knew what was going on, Celtic art had won the people's hearts and minds. Of course, no one could turn down the beauty of Celtic designs, even if they wanted to. Humans continue to enjoy Celtic masterpiece designs from pendants to rings, necklaces, tattoos, and other ornamental designs. Civilization might have shaped the kinds of knots being produced, but the Celtic culture remains intact.

Anyone who's determined and committed to learning the processes of Celtic art can create impressive Celtic knots. What if I don't have previous knowledge of art? No worries. You can learn the techniques. Again, this book uses easy-to-understand words to describe the process of creating excellent knots. So, you can learn the process from scratch once you're determined and committed.

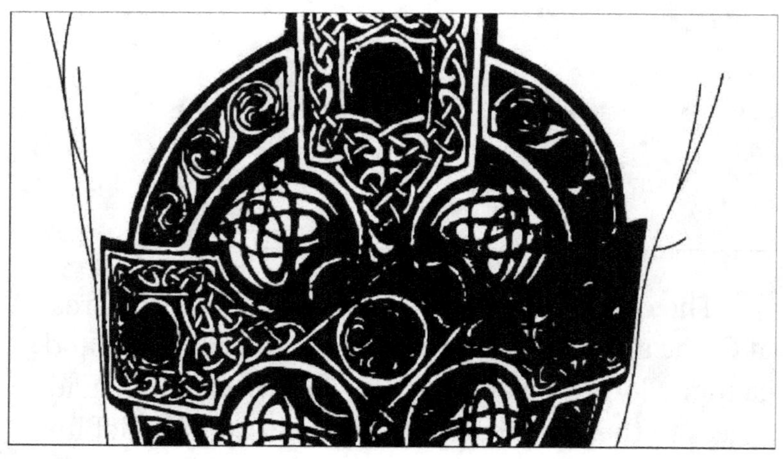

A career in Celtic art is full of positives. It is a platform to light up your creativity. Celtic art will open your eyes to innovative ways to light up your imagination. So, rather than idling your creativity, you can channel it into designing a fantastic Celtic pattern that will amaze many people. Also, it can show you a clearer picture of the world. A look at some Celtic designs and their supposed meanings will open your eyes to the realities of the world, and you'll learn so many things about other people's cultures and traditions through drawings. Still, Celtic art could be a path to fulfilling your passion. A career in Celtic art may not fetch you huge pay, but it could be an opportunity to follow your passion. Sure, it is something you'll love doing as soon as you get started.

What am I going to learn in this book?

So many amazing things to learn! Chapter one digs deep into the evolution of Celtic arts and the issues that aided the spread of the art during the Medieval period, while chapter two presents the gallery of beautiful Celtic ornaments and designs. Chapter three and four explains braids, twists, knotted lines, and Celtic patterns, with so many tips and tricks on how you can create your own designs at the comfort of your home.

Chapter five takes you through layout ideas and how to create one for your Celtic design. In chapter six, you will learn how to enhance your Celtic pattern with color, while chapter seven's focus is line enhancements. You may be dreaming of creating a unique and highly decorative Celtic design now. Great! Chapter eight offers the help you need to create a Celtic knot decorated, while chapter nine captures Celtic pattern knotted coasters.

Just name your questions. 'Celtic Patterns for Beginners' captures everything about Celtic art—yes, everything you need to be an established Celtic artist. Read, digest, and follow the techniques discussed in this book to create amazing Celtic patterns.

Chapter One: Introduction to Celtic Art

Celtic arts and crafts first hit Iron Age Europe around 1000 BCE, following a group of Celts migrating from Southern Russia. Early Celt migrants, who settled in the Upper Danube area, absorbed Ancient Danubian motifs and came with their cultural styles, including strings of knowledge from the Caucasian Bronze Age and the Mediterranean Etruscan styles. Still, they had vast experience in metalwork, jewelry art, and iron making. Their jewelry art, which was next to none at the time, could be from Russia's Caucasus' Bronze-making Maikop or as a result of Celts' early contact with the Levant. For example, the Gundestrup cauldron, Celts' masterpiece silver jewelry, was believed to hit the Black Sea region.

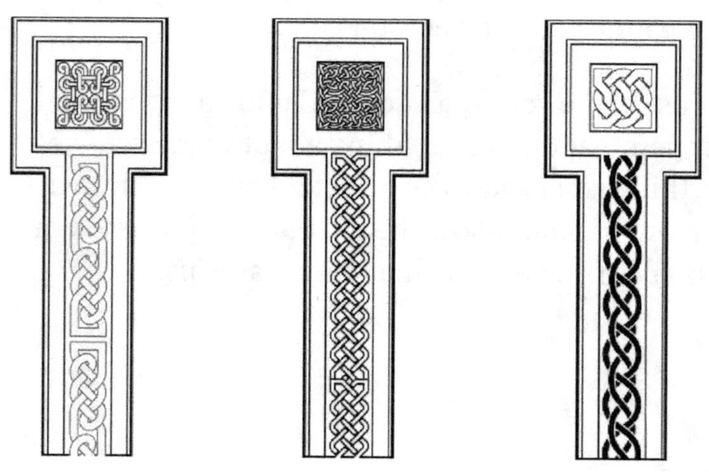

Celtic Art deals with lots of geometric shapes, and it covers several ornamental artistic designs such as patterns, spirals, and foliage. Following the revivalist movement to advance Celtic designs, the tentacles of Celtic Art were extended to cover other techniques and embellishments such as paintings, wall stenciling, stain glass, and different architectural designs. Ancient Celts were wealthy, intelligent, and complicated people. They were polytheists and very superstitious. Historically, most of them were farmers and warriors, and they lived on high mountains, where they could reverence natural elements such as the sun, the moon, the stars, and the Earth. Celts people believe that these natural elements could shape the course of their lives, either for good or bad. Apart from these natural elements, early Celtic Art designs also centered on another seven elements—plants, fish, reptiles, insects, birds, mammals, and humans.

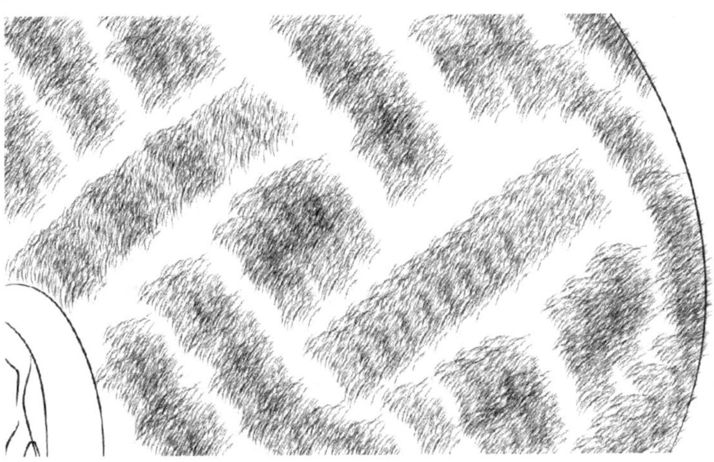

The Birth of Celtic Art

Historians contend that the Caucasians influenced early Celts during the Bronze Age. They believe that Celts' initial contact with the Caucasians helped them understand how to design iron and jewelry. Those things took center stage then. However, since the Celts traded with people close to the Mediterranean and the Black Sea, they might have been influenced by other art styles and cultures.

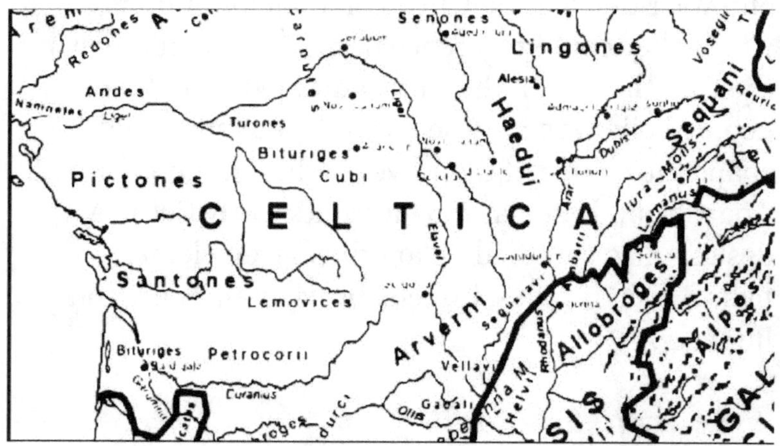

Still, the Celts learned a few things from the Danubian tradition. Artists soon learned to discard the classical tradition of Celtic Art by trading with people from other climes. Expectedly, the cultures and traditions of those people began to shape Celtic Arts. These influences snowballed into the various forms of designs we now see in Celtic knot patterns, scrollwork, letterings, and spirals. Celtic Art might have gone through many phases, but it's designs and patterns have always retained its intricate sense of balance.

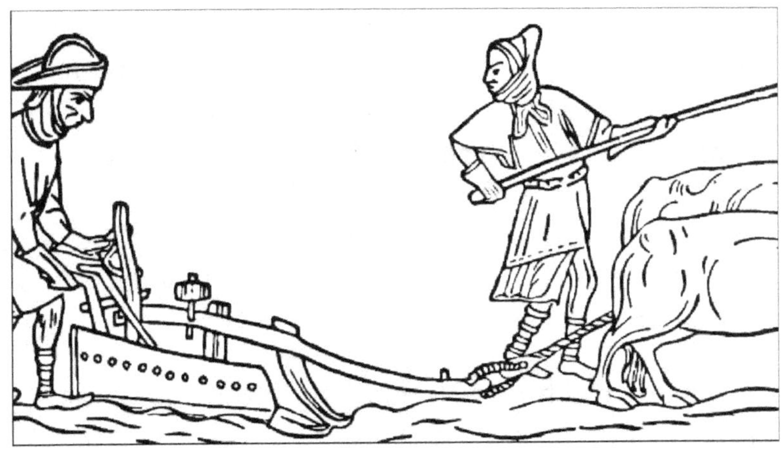

Celtic artists know how to balance positive and negative spaces to harmonize the message they intend to drive home. They try to elaborate their lines and curves to curb surface, vessel, and material irregularities, especially when they try to carve or draw Celtic patterns.

Early Celtic Art and La Tene

Nothing stood out in the early phase of Celtic Art more than its geometrical designs, lovely spirals, and charming active circles. Yet, those patterns and designs were previously unknown to Celtic Art. They were mostly wood carvings and metal sculptures from La Tene, a defunct region in present-day Switzerland. La Tene was the center of Iron Age culture in old Europe. Swirling curvilinear patterns and ornamental motifs were the standout designs of the Iron Age, and Artists in La Tene actively designed so many jewelry accessories with gold, bronze, iron, and other precious metals.

They also used these patterns to embellish their weapons, bowls, trumpets, cauldrons, and drinking vessels. Remember I told you that early Celts were mostly fighters and farmers. What we know as Celtic Art today is quite different from what was available hundreds of years before. Celtic Twilight, also known as the modern Celtic Art revival, has refined the Art to suit the present age.

The revival birthed a renewed interest in Celtic Art in the middle of the 19th century and paved the way for brooches and other unique Celtic designs. Also, Celtic motifs became dominant in architectural designs at this period. Still, knots, interlaced birds, whorls, and geometric designs, like other amazing Celtic art designs, flourished during this period.

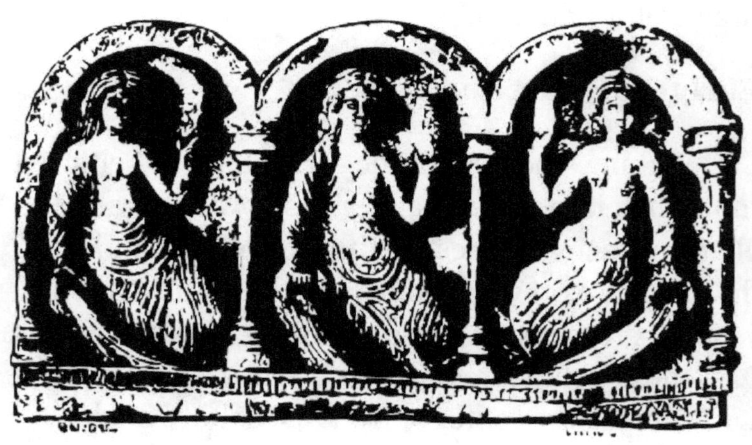

Celtic Knot Patterns

Celts were very religious and superstitious. They attached spiritual and superstitious meanings to most of their designs if not all. For example, Celtic mythology held that knots symbolized sacred geometry that connected life to the universe. Celtic knot patterns may vary, but they all represent one spiritual or superstitious thing or the other. Historians believe that Celtic knot patterns dated back to 450 A.D. when Christianity began to influence Celtic civilization. Some of these knot patterns, which symbolized love, friendship, faith, and loyalty, were used to design early Christian artworks and manuscripts.

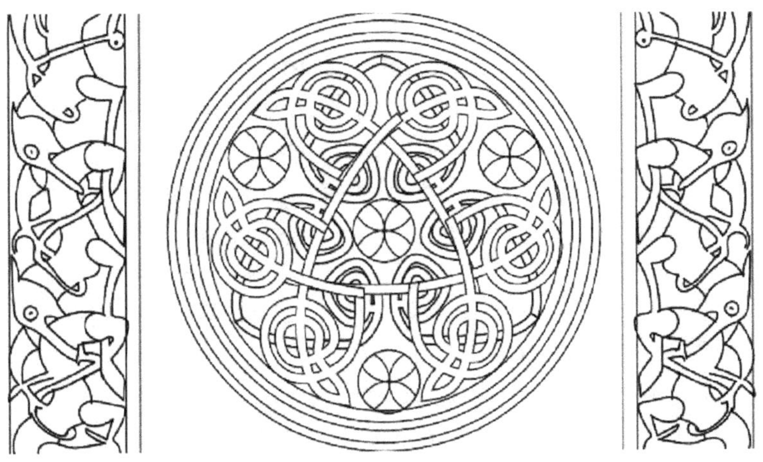

Still, intricate patterns were used, and still being used, to decorate items such as cutlery, clothing, plates, jewelry, and mugs. Some of these items are used daily, but many people still don't understand the symbolism and spirituality attached to these Celtic knot patterns. Regular Celtic knot patterns include the cross, trinity, tree of life, shield, heart, and spiral knots. Others are knotwork interlace, step patterns, and dara knots. Chapter Two captures all these knots, their meanings, and how you can create them.

Historical Overview of Interlocking and Interlacing Line Designs and Patterns

Interlace, a decorative art form in medieval Art, was a common visual art in the Iron Age. Artists looped and knotted bands and motifs to create complex geometric patterns. Those patterns were used to fill empty spaces in created designs. Norse Art of the Iron Age, Islamic Art, Insular Art of Ireland, and the Migration Art of Northern Europe extensively utilized interlacing. Intricate braided and interlaced patterns later made their way into Roman Art in many areas in Europe, especially in Mosaic floors. Then, the braided and interlaced patterns, also known as plaits in the United Kingdom, were widespread.

In the 5th and 6th century, Christians in Egypt used broad-strand ribbon interlace to decorate their Coptic manuscripts and textiles. The ornamental design looked like one of the earliest knotworks of insular Art. Yes, the insular Art of Ireland, as well as that of the British Isles.

Northern Europe was not left out. The Migration Period saw the birth of Style II, the animal style decoration. Interlace was at the center of this decoration, and it hit most parts of Northern Europe. Lombards eventually took the design to Northern Italy. The long ribbons of Style II terminated on the head of an animal. By 700 CE, the animal style decoration had begun to fade out in several areas in Europe, unlike Scandinavia and the British Isles.

In those areas, interlace was extensively used in woodcarving, metalwork, high crosses, runestones, and illuminated manuscripts. This development continued for five centuries—the 7th to 12th centuries. George Bain is an artist. He went through the Durham Cathedral Gospel Book and the Book of Durrow, books written in the 7th century. Having characterized the insular knotwork in the two books, George Bain found that broken and rejoined braids were extensively used. Still, no one knows how Coptic braid patterns got to the Hiberno-Scottish monasteries. But people tend to believe that the practices might have migrated from Lombardic Art in Italy or that of the Eastern Mediterranean.

James Johnson, an art historian, looked at it from another angle. He argued that the Coptic monasteries of Egypt and the Scriptoria of Early Christian in Ireland, being decorative interlace arts, deserved attention. Highlights of these two designs were their symmetrically-shaped and intertwined elongated beasts. Again, this design style dated back to the 7th century, and it is similar to the Hop and Sutton treasure. The Viking Age art, centered on the Urnes style, had the largest interlaced zoomorphic, and it dated as far back as 1050. The striking point of the Viking Age art was its stylized animals and intertwined tendrils of foliate designs.

The British Isles' insular Art activated the full flowering of interlace in Northern Europe. Style II, Northern Europe's animal style ornament, was blended with ribbon knotwork designs found in the Cross of Cong and the Book of Kells, two great books of the time. Christian activities strongly influenced those books. Interlace was used to illuminate carpet pages and other notable designs of the time. Soon, insular interlace found its way into continental Europe and was extensively used between the 8th and 11th centuries. Franco-Saxon school and Carolingian schools of illumination, like other notable schools of the time, utilized interlace in their foliate decorative designs. Also, Romanesque Art was no different. Less complex interlace patterns and animal designs were found.

Interlace patterns formed the highlight of Islamic Art. Islamic ornament had lots of geometric interlacing patterns. Most of these patterns fell under arabesque designs and were evident in Umayyad architecture designs such as cravings and wall paintings, mosaics, decorative metalwork, and window grilles. Such techniques took center stage in Islamic Art between the 8th and 10th centuries but later paved the way for the intricate interlacing patterns of medieval Islamic Art. Kufic calligraphy also had some interlaced elaborations.

Southern Europe, just like the Northern part, had its fair share in the historical evolution of interlacing. Byzantine Art, the region's known design, was impacted by interlace and knotwork, although with little or no prominence. Three-ribbon, the only notable example of interlace in the area, was found in Croatia in the early medieval period. The interlace was carved on stone between the 9th and 11 centuries.

Chapter Summary

- Celtic art hit Iron Age Europe in 1000 BCE.

- It covers ornamental artistic designs as spirals and foliage and can be used for geometric shapes.

- The tentacles of Celtic art can be extended to other forms of designs and embellishments.

In the next chapter, you will learn a few things about Celtic art Gallery.

Chapter Two: Gallery

We already considered the meaning and history of Celtic arts and patterns in the last chapter. Let's take a step further to see a few examples of Celtic designs and create some projects. So, one after the other, let us run through these Celtic patterns. Celtic knots are usually bold, adorable, and appealing, but they all have unique meanings, all parts of the Celtic heritage. Each Celtic symbol has a particular purpose or message, although this meaning may vary across cultures.

Today, we will go back to history to study these Celtic symbols and their meanings carefully. So, sit comfortably, relax while I take you around the world of Celtic symbols.

Trinity Knot

The Trinity knot is also known as Triquetra. It was the symbol of the Mother, Maiden, and Crone, a famous Celts' goddess. It is one of the most popular Celtic characters.

The Trinity knot is highly symbolic and has a deep spiritual meaning, especially among the Irish. For some, it is believed to be a symbol of the 'Holy Trinity' representing God – The Father, The Son, and The Holy Spirit.

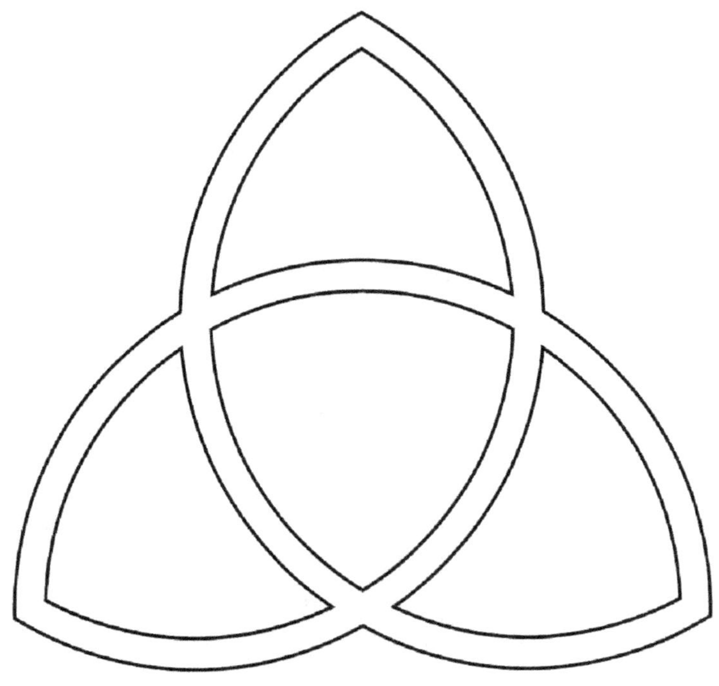

In Christendom, especially among Catholics, representations of the Trinity knot are found on paintings and artworks on the church walls. Among neo-pagan worshippers, the Trinity knot also holds significance. It signifies the three-life cycles of womanhood in relation (Youth, Motherhood, and Old Age) to the moon's phases – past, present, and future.

The Trinity Knot is a typical Celtic design replicated on jewelry, artwork, and other medieval art forms. The Celtic Trinity Knot is worn by many Irish as a symbol of never-ending love or ancestry.

You should also know that the Trinity Knot holds several meanings, and some of these include:

- The Trinity knot is also referred to as the Irish Love Knot.

- As a gift, it connotes a wish of the longevity of life to the receiver.

- According to ancient beliefs, Trinity Knot also symbolizes the three phases of a woman: Youth, Motherhood, and Old age.

- The endless intertwining curves found in most Trinity knots usually symbolizes everlasting love and is an excellent gift for engagements, weddings, and marriage anniversaries.

- The Trinity knot also symbolizes the three circles of life: life, death, and rebirth.

- It also represents the husband's marital vows to his wife: love, honor, and protection.

- It also symbolizes the moon phases, which has to do with time - past, present, and future; or the family structure representing the father, mother, and children.

- It is a representation of ancient Irish culture.

Celtic Self-Contained Patterns

These are twists, braids, and knot patterns created using one continuous line to create an aesthetic Celtic design. Celtic self-contained patterns are usually without a beginning or end, i.e., there is no starting or finishing point on a Celtic knot. These are mainly used for decorations.

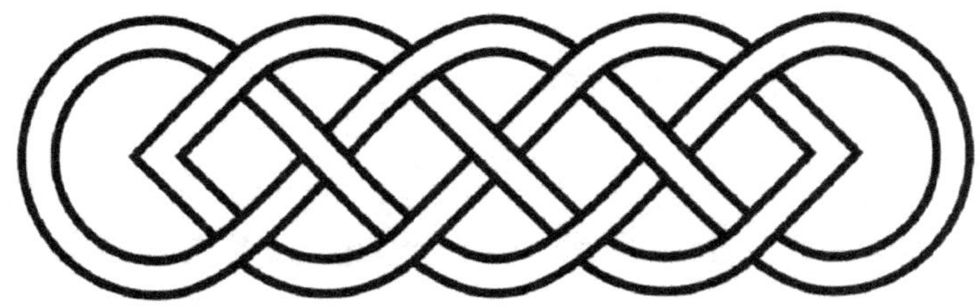

Celtic step patterns and critical patterns are prevalent motifs found in ancient Celtic arts right before the Christian influence on the Celts. However, these Celtic designs found their way into early Christian manuscripts and artwork.

Step patterns are also known as maze patterns and were found in ancient Egypt, Aztec, and Mayan art. It can symbolize progression and motion. It could also connote the spiritual relationship between heaven and earth.

Some of these artworks, in addition to depictions from life, such as animals, plants, and even humans, have been replicated over time by famous artists and painters.

Cutting Instructions (cut in the order listed)

- White/green print (background

- 4 rectangles 3½" x 6½"

- 1 square 3½" x 3½"

- 4 squares 2" x 2"

Dark green swirl print, medium lime mottle, light green floral, and dark green texture (links)—cut from each:

- 1 strip 2" x 5"

- 1 rectangle 2" x 3½"

- 3 squares 2" x 2"

Piecing the Block.

1. Sew together 1 white/green print 2" square, 1 dark green swirl print 2" square, and 1 medium lime mottle 2" x 3½" rectangle to make pieced square.

2. Make 4 total in fabric arrangements shown.

3. Draw a diagonal line on the wrong side of lime 2″ square. Place marked square on white/green 3½" x 6½" rectangle, right sides together, aligning raw edges.

4. Stitch on the drawn line and trim away.

Celtic Spiral Knot

The Celtic Spiral Knot is a representation of infinity, and it symbolizes unity and union of spirit. It represents the human journey from the physical to spiritual life/phase.

The Spiral Knot was mostly found at graveyards, often engraved on tombs. Thus, it is thought to be a symbol of the human transition from life to death.

The most common type of Spiral Knot that you'd find is the Triple Spiral Knot, which is also a trinity design, and three connecting spirals often represent it. They represent the water, fire, and earth, which are the driving force of nature.

Types of Celtic Spirals

Single Spiral

You may not know, but the single spiral is one of the most common Celtic symbols found on monuments and other artifacts. It holds different meanings, and for some people, it could stand for growth, equity, affinity, order, and development.

For others, it could represent the mind's journey from a materialistic world to an astronomical/cosmic world. It is also a competent representation of knowledge, experiences, and mindfulness.

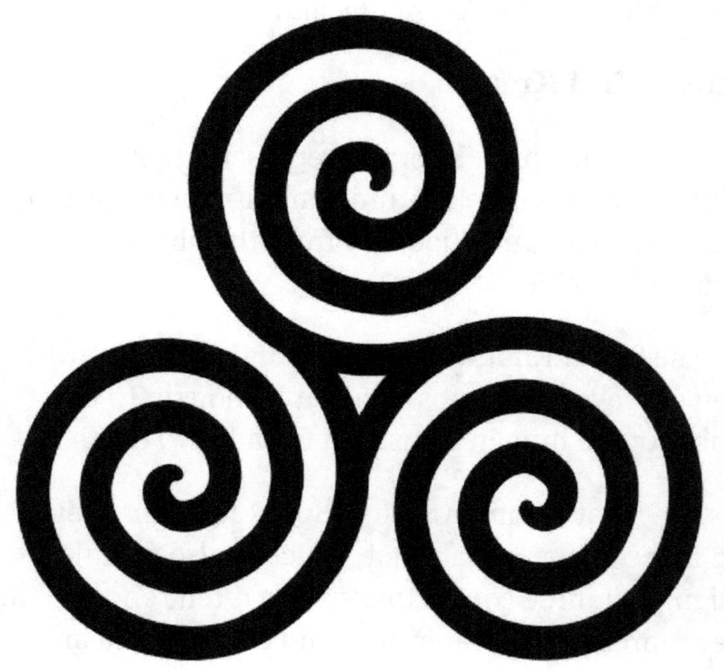

Double Spiral

The Double Spiral is a clockwise movement of two points on a line that forms the double spiral. Just like the single spiral, it also has various meanings for different people. According to ancient beliefs, the double spiral symbolizes the sun and its double spiral movement, which happens over a year.

It could also represent balance and is also a symbol that represents man's creation and destruction, human birth, death, and a profound spiritual awakening.

Triple Spiral

Also referred to as the Triple Spiralis, the Triple Spiral is an ancient Celtic symbol that became very popular in 500BC. The versatility of the triple spiral meanings cannot be overemphasized; although it depends on the context and culture, it is used.

It could represent progress, revolution, movement, cycle, etc. It could also stand for the soul, body, and mind. Also, it symbolizes intellect, love, and power. It also represents the physical, spiritual, and cosmic world.

Celtic Love Knot

This type of Celtic knot, also called the Trikeles, represents undying and everlasting love between two people. The Celtic Love knot is also referred to as the Anam Cara Knot. From the Irish words meaning soul friend, it was recently added to the list of Celtic Knots.

Here, two Celtic knot hearts are intertwined to form one infinite loop, and it is a modern acclimation of the classic Celtic knot. One thing you should know is that the pattern found on the Celtic Love Knot is infinite.

It is common among lovers and is used to represent a relationship of everlasting love. You can find most lovers wearing rings with the Love knot pattern, and in ancient marriage rites, lovers exchanged this knot instead of rings.

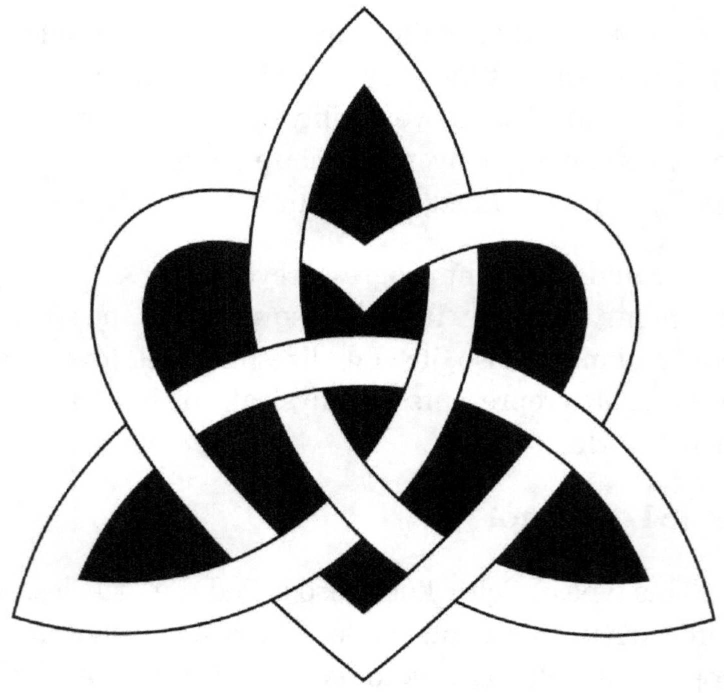

Celtic Cross

The Celtic Cross stands for the four elements and directions according to ancient legends. The Celtic Cross was and is still highly a religious and spiritual symbol. The Celtic ornate cross holds a lot of meaning for both pagans and Christians.

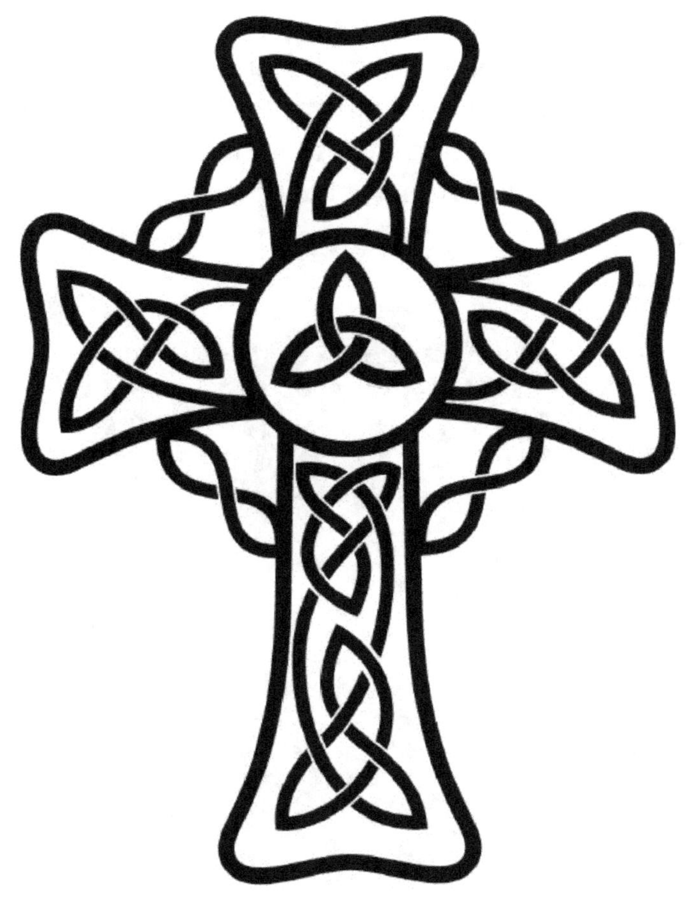

For pagans, the circle found at the center of the cross references the Sun God in ancient times. On the other hand, Christians believe that the cross was where Jesus Christ, the son of God, died for our sins; hence, it symbolizes God's love, which is eternal.

Round Celtic Design

The Round Celtic Design is one of the most popular Celtic symbols. Many people believe that the symbol is a representation of the Christian teachings of the Holy Trinity. Hence it connotes the unity of spirit.

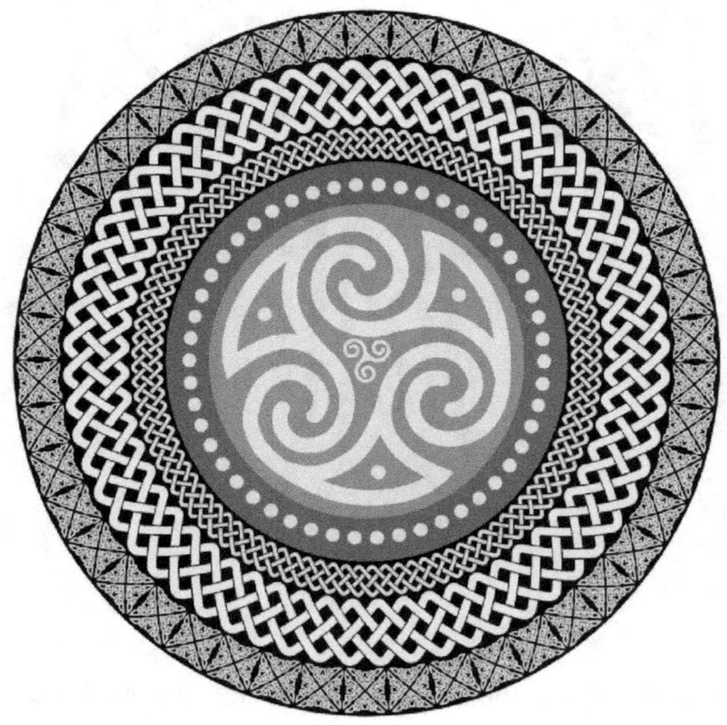

Among Christians, there is the belief that the circle symbolizes God's never-ending love and a representation of the cycle of life, which is birth, death, and rebirth. It also stands for loyalty, friendship, and love, although these meanings may vary among different cultures.

Frame Corner

The Frame corner is also a well-known Celtic design that is very aesthetic. It is an ancient Celtic design made on frames for embellishments. A frame corner doesn't have any known meaning or symbolism; however, it is a modern addition to the collection of classic Celtic designs and patterns.

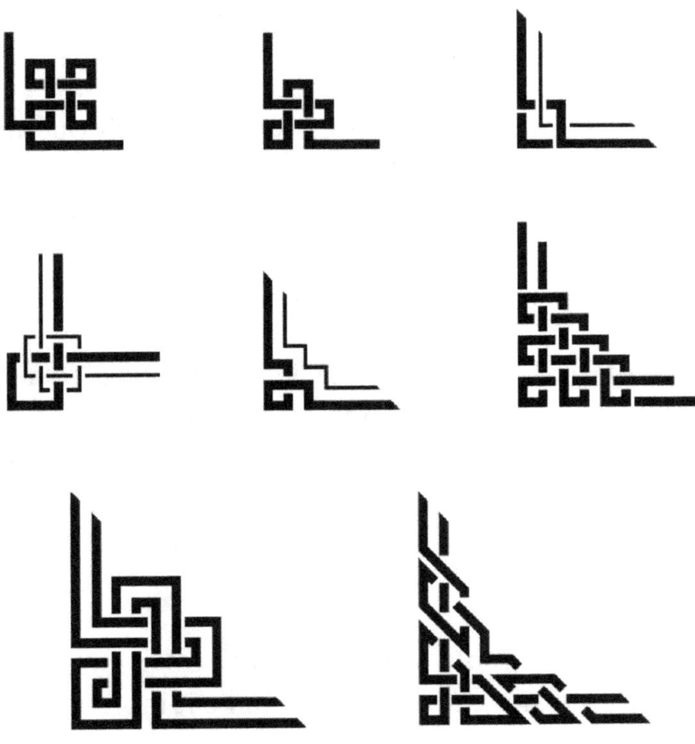

To create a Celtic frame corner is relatively easy once you follow guidelines thoroughly. You need to get your glue, quick clamps, a poplar board, glazier points, wood stain, straight router and round bit, miter saw, and a flush-trim saw.

Here are the guidelines on how to create your frame corner:

1. Using a 1x4 poplar board, cut out 4 boards and rip them down to 3 inches each.

2. Make accurate cuts on your boards by using your miter saw set to 45 degrees.

3. After making your cut, lay your boards out and check for errors. Once that is done, apply your glue to each board and join them together, making sure they're all square and clamped tightly together using your quick clamps.

4. After applying the glue, you can choose to add corner splines to your board. To do this, you make use of a DIY spline jig and a contrasting wood. Cut out another set of poplar boards, add glue, and push your spline into the boards' joints.

5. You can apply wood finishings to give your frame an extra shine and make it more pleasing to the eyes.

6. Trim off rough edges and extra wood using your flush trim saw.

7. Assemble your frame by using glazier points to hold everything in place, especially when screwing your corner splines. You should screw every 6 inches (a bit more or less) using a Flathead screwdriver.

Just like that, you have completed the Celtic frame corner.

Square Knot

The square knot is also known as the shield knot. It was an ancient Celtic Knot that was worn by warriors for protection in times of war. Ill people also used it to ward off illness and evil spirits, and danger.

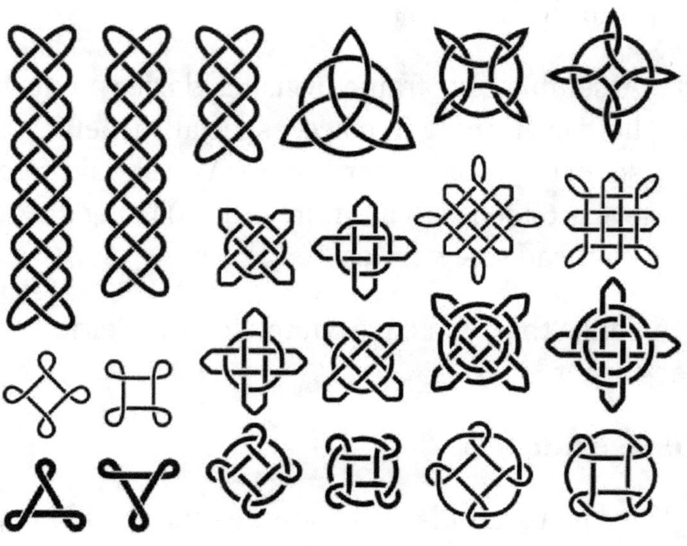

You can recreate the Square or shield knot in various designs. However, you must include its four corners to make it a square knot. The square knot comprises heavily-made patterns that are tight to depict an unbreakable barrier.

The shield knot has a lot of complex meanings. It can symbolize the elements of nature, which are earth, wind, fire, and water. Also, it represents St. Brigid's four tiers of wisdom, i.e., heart, head, hearth, and hand.

The square knot represents good fortune and prosperity and the four unique Celtic festivals - Imbolic, Samhain, Lughnasadh, and Bealtaine.

Circular Knot

Circular knots usually come in different designs, although one thing they share in common is that they are all circular. Circular knots often symbolizes the continuity of human life and also purity and wholeness.

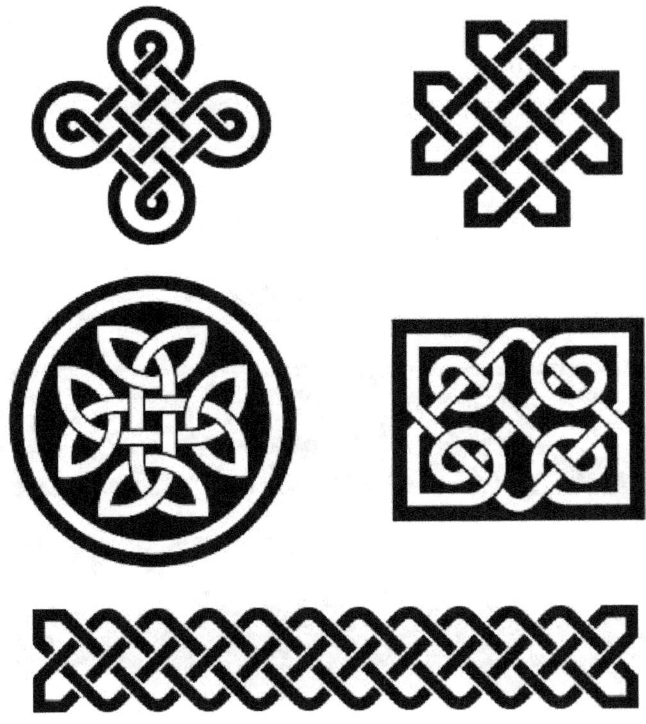

There is no beginning or end in circular knots, which is common among almost all Celtic knots. The Dara knot, which is almost like a maze, is an example of a Celtic circular knot, and they symbolize leadership, power, wisdom, and strength. Dara's name comes from the Irish word 'Doire,' meaning oak tree, which represents strength.

Knot Birds Designs

Animals were an essential part of Celtic folklore and mythology. Ancient Celtic legends often associated animals with motion, fertility, and vitality. Out of all the animals, the most common one depicted in Celtic mythology and arts was the Bird. The Celts had a peculiar connection with birds.

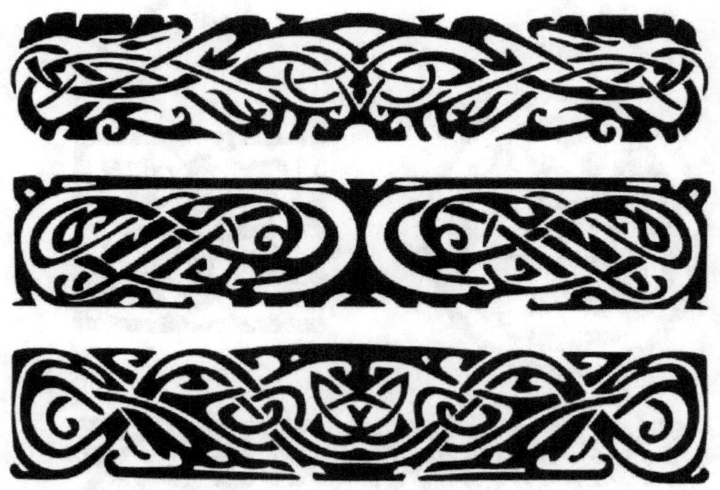

When you come across most images of ancient Celtic and Druid gods, you see that the artist depicted these gods holding birds in their hands who acted as divine servants.

In ancient Celtic arts and beliefs, birds symbolized skill, knowledge, and, weirdly, bloodshed. Hence, old Celtic artists drew on the shields of most Celtic warriors and other emblems. The most commonly depicted birds are the swan, crow, and raven, although other animals were not left out. Old Celtic chiefs believed these birds were divine messengers of the gods, and because of this, they were revered.

The crow and raven usually represented bloodshed and battle, as well as connoting prophecy too. The Celtic 'triple' goddess, Morrigan, who controlled fertility, birth, and even death, is associated with the raven. The Celts used the raven to symbolize the death of slain warriors and also depict darkness. Even in modern movies and art, the raven still has a dark undertone and meaning to it, as you must have noticed.

The knot bird design holds different meanings. In ancient times, the Celts used birds to describe a warrior's fighting skills and prowess. It is also used to depict strength and was popular in ancient times.

Solomon's Knot

It is a Celtic symbol that represents man's connection to the divine. It is associated with King Solomon and reminiscent of many ancient civilizations apart from the Celts.

Awen Knot

It symbolizes creative inspiration and is associated with the poet, Bards.

Brigid's Cross

Early Christians named Brigid's cross after St. Brigid. People used Brigid's cross as a form of protection from evil spirits and danger. In Ireland, the Brigid cross also symbolizes the beginning of spring.

The Sailor's Knot

Ancient Celtic sailors weaved this to remember the loved ones they had left at home. It also represents everlasting love.

Celtic Tree of Life

The Celtic Tree of Life is a symbol of strength, balance, and harmony. The Celts believed that the dead lived in trees when they died, so they revered trees because it was a link between the living and the dead.

Chapter Summary

- Trinity knot is the symbol of The Mother, Maiden, and Crone.

- It symbolizes everlasting love and can be given to someone who's special to you.

The next chapter captures braids, twists, and knotted lines. Hope to see you there soon!

Chapter Three: Introduction to Braids, Twists, and Knotted Lines

Braids, twists and knotted lines add beauty to quilts. They make our designs attractive and adorable. In this chapter, we will look at some of them and try to create some.

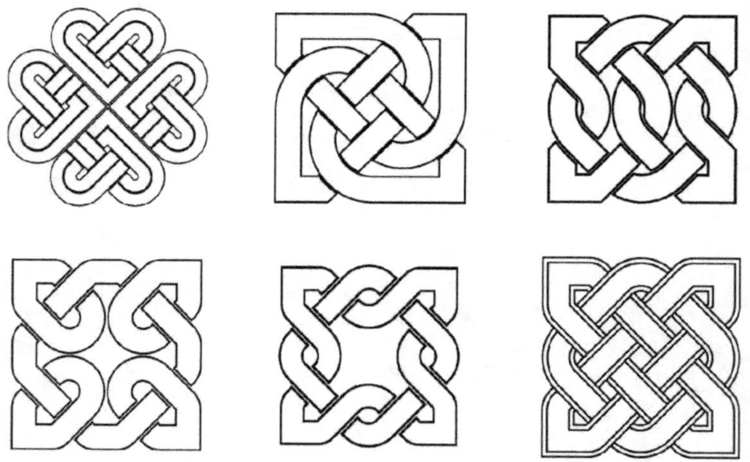

How to Draw a Celtic Cross

The Celtic Cross can be used to design beautiful pendants, jewelry, and rings, apart from other notable projects. Most often, and because of its spiritual undertone, Christians tend to use items decorated with this Cross more than other religious adherents. Why? The Celtic cross symbolizes the Cross on which

Jesus Christ was crucified. Here, I will teach you how to draw the Cross at the comfort of your home.

Required Materials

- Graph or grainy paper

- Pencil and eraser

- Pen or marker

- Ruler

Instructions

Follow these simple steps to draw your own Celtic Cross.

Step 1: Start by sketching the circle that will frame the center of the knot.

Step 2: Sketch a small circle that corresponds with the initial sketch.

Step 4: Sketch another smaller circle in the center of the already drawn circles

Step 5: Sketch the limbs of the Celtic knot. Sketch a set of parallel bent lines that deviate from one another on the side of the smallest center circle.

Join these lines on each end to make a scalloped style by linking numerous slight bent lines. Sketch a little L-shaped line above the center of each limb.

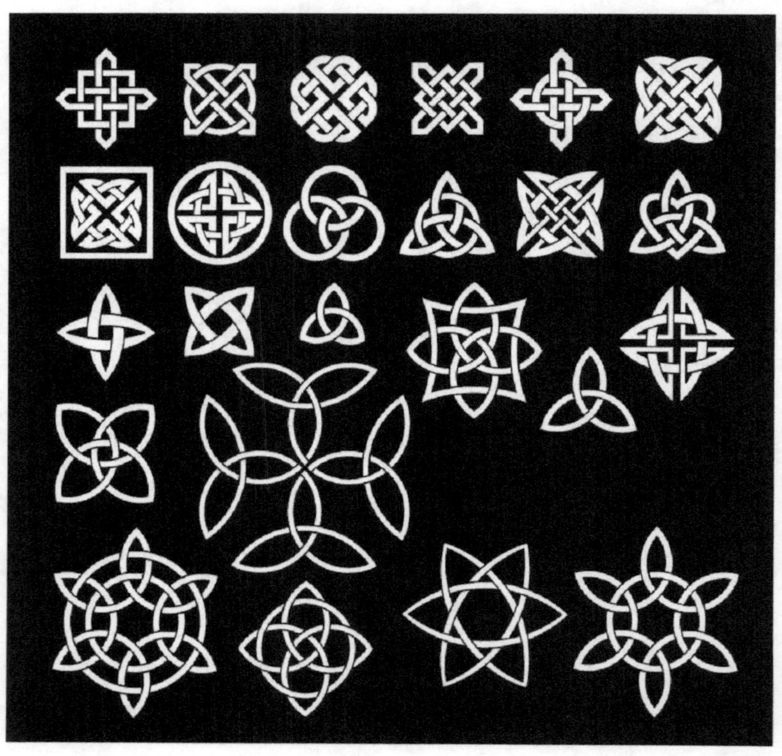

How to Draw a Trinity Knot

Trinity knot looks beautiful and charming. It is the perfect knot for Christians since it symbolizes 'The Father, The Son, and The Holy Spirit.' The knot has been extensively used to create lots of beautiful projects like rings, pendants, and necklaces. Also, these projects are what you can design in the comfort of your home once you know how to draw the trinity knot. No worries. Here, I will guide you on how you can draw your own trinity knot.

Required Materials

- Graph paper

- Pencil

- An eraser

- Pen or marker

- Ruler

Instructions

Follow these simple steps to draw your own trinity knot.

Step 1: Draw a separating line, and place a dot at the lower part of left and right. Place another dot at the upper part of the left and right.

Step 2: Sketch a big curve beginning from the top dot, curving to the right of the separator, then move over to the left-hand dot.

Step 3: Sketch another curve from the top dot, downward to the left of the separator, and then over to the right-hand dot.

Step 4: Connect the left and right dots with a curve bent to the top in the center. Thus, the outside shape of the trinity knot is complete.

Step 5: Now sketch another trinity knot line inside the first line. Make sure the width is equal.

How to Draw a Tree of Life

Another striking Celtic symbol is the tree of life, bold, beautiful, adorable, and unique. It has a few spiritual meanings, like other forms of Celtic patterns. Remember that Celts were highly religious people, and they had a way of linking their designs to religion. Learning how to draw the Celtic tree is fun since you can use it to embellish your projects. Good. So, I will now show you how to draw the tree with little or no assistance. Are you ready?

Materials Required

- Graph paper

- Pencil and eraser

- Pen or marker

- Ruler

- Compass

Instructions

Follow these simple steps to draw your own Celtic tree of life pattern.

Step 1: Begin With two curved sides of the tree to perfectly bend the upper curve twigs.

Step 2: Sketch the lower line and twigs.

Step 3: Insert two new center twigs.

Step 4: Move to the base, insert smaller twigs.

Step 5: Insert more smaller twigs.

Step 6: Insert ornamental shapes such as triangles.

Step 7: Insert decorations to the base.

Step 8: Indicate with a pointer and color with crayons.

How to Draw a Celtic Heart Knot

The heart symbolizes love. The Celtic heart is a gift of love. It is a design for someone you genuinely love and value—maybe your girlfriend or fiancé. Although the pattern is quite simple to draw, some quilters still have issues getting it right. Why? You're going to end up with something else if you miss a dot or a line. No worries. I will show you how to draw it perfectly, and you'll be producing a fantastic Celtic

heart knot right there in your home. Here is how to
design your Celtic heart knot.

Materials Required

- Graph paper

- Pencil and eraser

- Pen or marker

- Ruler

- Compass

Instructions

Follow these simple steps to draw your own Celtic
heart knot.

Step 1: Just like the name indicates, draw out a
heart and make sure you join both sides to form a
diamond where the two ends meet at the top.

Step 2: Exploiting the lines for the diamond,
design three linking lines. The three lines must curve a
little bit.

Step 3: At the outer part of the heart drawn
initially, draw another heart.

Step 4: At this time, when the two lines meet in
the middle at the top, the line on the right goes
straight down to the first heart, and the line on the left

stops at the line on the right. Inside the heart itself, draw in the lines as shown to complete the lines that are already there to show them overlapping.

Step 5: Complete them by tracing the same line until you form three arrow-like points. Only the line on the right should overlap the heart in the center on each one of them.

Step 6: When you erase all the red lines, this is what you are left with. Make sure there are no breaks in the lines and that none of the lines are perfectly straight and you are totally finished.

How to Draw a Celtic Spiral

Celtic spiral is a charming design. It is bold and attractive. The Celtic spiral could be single, double, or triple, but all of them can beautify your quilts. Although there are variations on how you design the three spiral patterns, what I'll be sharing with you here will help you master Celtic spirals. Fine. Just pay keen attention to what we have here, and nothing will stop you from creating your Celtic spiral right there in your home.

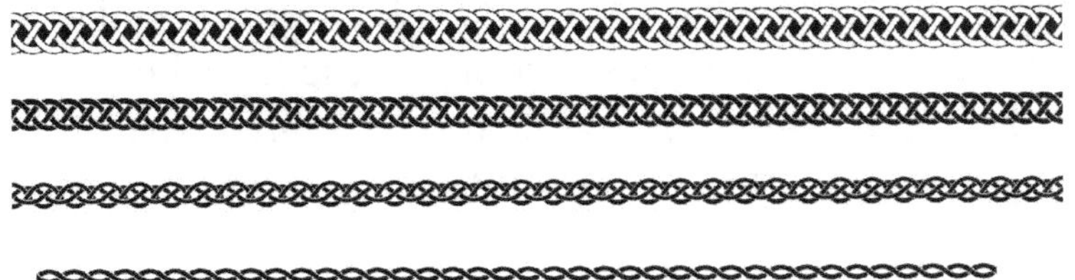

Materials Required

- Graph paper

- Pencil and eraser

- Pen or marker

- Ruler

Instructions

Follow these simple steps to design your own Celtic spiral.

Step 1: Begin the spiral with a circle with your compass placed one inch apart. Sketch another circle at the middle of the paper with your compass set at two inches apart.

Step 2: Sketch another circle with your compass set at three inches.

Note: you can increase your compass to four inches and even five inches, depending on the size of your drawing material.

Step 3: Sketch two lines across the circles all the way through your circles. Let one of the lines be upward and the other be downward. Sketch two "X" shape-like lines across the circles.

Step 4: Start to sketch a spiral. Each spiral should contain at least two or three curved angles.

Draw an "X" in each of these spirals to join the bottom left corner with the upper right.

Step 5: Finish the spiral. You should sketch eight lines that form spirals in each direction. These spirals should be both clockwise and anti-clockwise. Sketch the spiral again in a curve way. Then, spread the curved line into the center of the angle.

How to Draw Knotted Lines

With knotted lines, you can take your designs to higher heights. These lines are just too charming and beautiful to neglect. They can make your designs irresistible, and you'll love the outlook of your Celtic knot. Yet, creativity is required if you want to create a lovely and appealing knotted line. Don't worry. I will take you through the process of designing these lines.

Required Materials

- Graph paper

- Pencil and eraser

- Pen or marker

- Lightbox (optional)

- Contrasting colored pen or marker (optional)

- Unlined paper (optional)

Instructions

Follow these steps to draw your own knotted line with a graph.

Step 1: Sketch the Grid: First, sketch a zigzag grid with an even number of lines and columns—count two squares for each column and row—for example, 6 columns by 6 rows. Columns and rows can easily be counted using dots along the edges. Most times, your columns and your rows may not be the same. You can have 4 columns by 8 rows grid. Although there is no limit to the number of columns or rows you can have.

Step 2: Draw some Vertical and Horizontal Lines: Sketch few vertical and horizontal lines at any point you want. The line must contain an even number of squares and dots placed at the center of the line. Your creativity is needed here. Every line you created should lean towards your Celtic knot.

Step 3: Connect the Dots: Join all your dots with diagonal lines. Your vertical or horizontal lines drawn earlier should not be joined with any other lines. Complete the joining of the dots by sketching a curve between the dots near your vertical and horizontal lines. Note the interaction between the knot and the line drawn. It will allow you to get loops, waves, and corners in your knot.

Reduce the gaps by outlining over alternating dots as you trace the line of your knot. Find the meeting points in the lower-left corner. Connect the meeting point by tracing over that dot. Sketch over one, skip one, sketch over the next, and so on.

Step 4: Make it Fancy: You can make your knot look extra beautiful by widening or tightening up the gaps. This technique will make it look like a continuous rope. To make this, use a pen of different colors and draw lines on each side. Don't be too concerned about the gap of the point but make sure it is the same. Since you know the secret, I believe you can configure your own Celtic knot now and understand the size of all types of knots.

Uses of the Celtic Knot Design

The uses of Celtic knot designs are many. Let start by looking at creative art, jewelry, clothing, and home decoration. You will understand that Celtic knot designs are integrated into all of these areas. This alone can make wedding rings and other jewelry look beautiful.

Celtic knot designs are commonly imprinted or decorated into leather to make pocketbooks, wallets, and clothing materials. The art of inscription is enabled heavily by the use of Celtic knot designs. It is also employed alongside the sides of the page and as initial letters of paragraphs. It can sometimes even show up in the middle of sentences to emphasize a point or an idea. Learning to design and draw Celtic knots can add a new dimension to whatever art form you choose.

Some knots can be used for decorative purposes, while others are used for deeper purposes with in-depth meaning.

Some Celtic families used to have their own knot for refrain and entertainment, this allowed them to customize it easily, and it is known to the family alone. Of course, there were also knots in Celtic that carry the same meaning and symbol for everyone. This includes the spiral knot or the sailor's knot.

The spread of Christianity made it forbidden for Celts and other heathens to practice their faith. The Celts found a way around this by hiding small Celtic elements in their stories. They also integrated the knots in Christian artwork.

Countless numbers of knots can also be found on gravestones, churches, and manuscripts, where these Celtic knots were used to beautify letters. In crosses, the knotwork is also used in addition to Biblical stories. For example, the Celtic cross is made with ornamentation of Celtic knots.

Drawing Celtic Knot Designs

To make use of Celtic knot designs, you must be able to sketch them as decorations. There are a few methods that can help you improve your knowledge on this.

Graph Paper Method

This may require you to use graph paper and Ink for the sketching. This is for the Beginners. Sketching by hand is seen as time-consuming, but the best way to draw Celtic knots by some purists. You will sketch a rectangle on the graph paper, which contains an odd number of angles in both length and width. All odd numbers are allowed. Then input dots to each corner of the rectangle and every other square on each side.

Make use of multiple colored pencils, sketch a dot on the next line inside your original rectangle. Avoid sketching the second of dots at the corners. When you have finished putting the rectangle of dots inside the original rectangle, you will draw slanting lines from the inside dot to the other inside dot, beginning with the top left.

Then go to the top right and draw diagonal lines again from inside dot to inside dot. It helps to use a ruler during this step to keep your guidelines perfectly straight. When you have finished connecting the inside dots going both directions, you will have created a grid that can be used to create your Celtic knot design. By using curving lines and straight lines in a balanced fashion on the grid, you can create many beautiful and unique Celtic knots.

Computer-Drawn Celtic Knot Designs

Most people are not interested in the old way of drawing Celtic knot designs. There are several other ways to use computer programs to sketch Celtic knot designs. Computer programs, such as Adobe Illustrator, allow you to test and try out with color quickly and easily. Computer programs will enable you to copy a design section and repeat it as often as you would like. This process hastens the job and makes it look neat and simple. This style also enables you to create big, complex, and sophisticated Celtic knot designs quickly. Other drafting programs, such as AutoCAD, can be used to design the knotwork and do Celtic jewelry mockups.

Celtic knot designs are attractive and gorgeous. They contain a rich cultural and historical background and legacy. Celtic knot designs are symbolic and carry meaning inside meaning and many complex ideas. Knowing how to draw Celtic knot designs manually or through computer system programs may look frightening or discouraging. Still, it can be done by anyone interested and who wants to put effort into doing it. The result of that effort will be a whole new design aspect to add to your art or craft. Celtic knots can add a unique flair to jewelry, leather, cloth, calligraphy, or even tattoo designs.

Chapter Summary

- Braids, twists, and knotted lines are used to beautify quilts.

- The Celtic cross is used to design pendants, jewelries, and rings.

In the next chapter, you will learn about Celtic patterns.

Chapter Four:
Celtic Patterns

Celtic patterns are highly intricate knots and graphical images of knots that serve mainly as aesthetics and decoration, originating from Celtic art. These knots are popular because of how widely used and represented in Christian monuments and manuscripts. Examples of these are found in the Book of Kells, the Lindisfarne Gospels, and the 8th- century St. Teilo Gospels.

Most Celtic patterns are endless knots and appear in various varieties of basket weave knots.

How to Draw a Line and Border Patterns

Drawing a line and border pattern is relatively easy, but you need to pay attention when drawing your grid and pattern so that it comes out correctly. Just follow these simple steps to design your own line and border pattern.

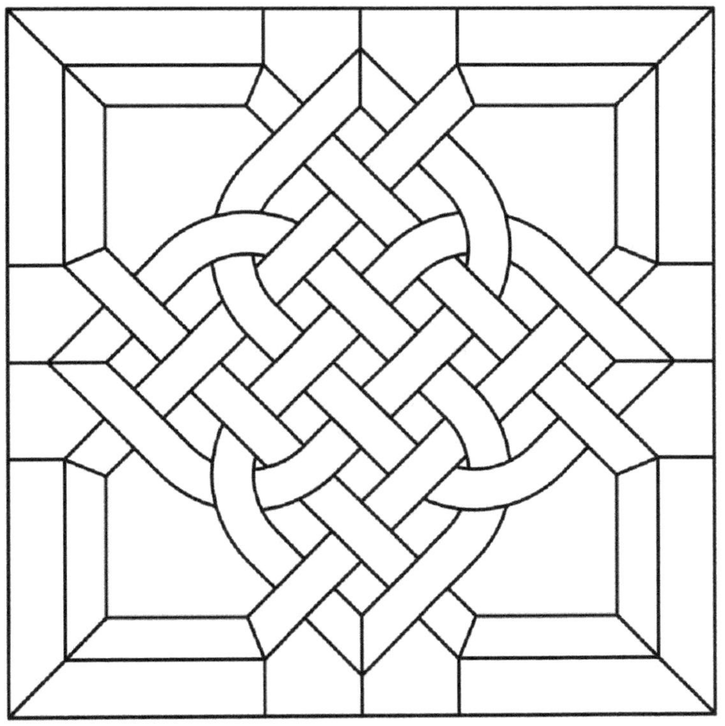

Step 1: As a beginner, use a grid. It is best to use a big grid because it makes drawing the pattern easier.

Step 2: Put the grid under your drawing paper and trace the grid to create a border. A rectangle is better and more comfortable.

Step 3: Start drawing your squares inside the grid and squares around from the four corners of the grid and work your way towards the center of the paper.

Step 4: Continue drawing under, over, and under alternatively and repeat the process for about 500 times till you get one giant knot.

Step 5: Try to keep your lines symmetrical. Draw your lines again to make them appear bolder and straighter. You can use a coloring pencil to add more color to your knot.

Step 6: You could always switch styles by making more or fewer corners, make a double border with a frame, add colors, circles, etc.

The goal is to have fun while creating your line and border pattern.

How to Make a Corner Pattern

A corner pattern can aid the aesthetics of your Celtic knot. It is beautiful if it is well-crafted. Some designers often complain that the corner pattern is a bit complex, but you have nothing to worry about. Here, I will teach you how to create a corner pattern in the comfort of your home.

Required Materials

- Graph paper

- Colored pencils

- Marker

- An eraser

Instructions

Follow these simple steps to design your corner pattern.

Step 1: Place your basic units in a string and connect each unit with curves.

Step 2: Use a simple or complex corner unit to connect your unit seamlessly.

Step 3: End the string you made with an end unit using half your string's width.

Step 4: Shade your units with a pencil to add shadows to overlapped bands. Keep the width of your bands equal.

Step 5: Connect the bands that face the outside border.

Step 6: Start with forming basic units. Connect The tops and bottoms of each unit with curves. Connect the middle ends with straight lines. Ensure the bands that start on top - go under, the bands that begin below - go above.

Step 7: Create a knot in each corner to tangle your bands.

Step 8: Turn one of your bands into a curve that ends on the axis. Your curve can take any shape.

Step 9: Your outside curve should be the same as the first one and go through the same key point on the axis.

Step 10: Extend the other band into a different curve, add width, and ensure they end on the same axis.

Step 11: Interweave all line units you've drawn and erase every part that appears overlapped.

Step 12: Erase all pencil marks and use a marker to outline.

Step 13: Shade your unit when you are done to smooth, blend, and create a realistic drop shadow effect.

How to Draw Celtic Circles and Squares

Celtic circles and squares can make your Celtic knotwork beautiful and charming. Just design these circles and squares with creativity, and you'll love the final output. How do I create my Celtic circles or squares? No worries. Here is how.

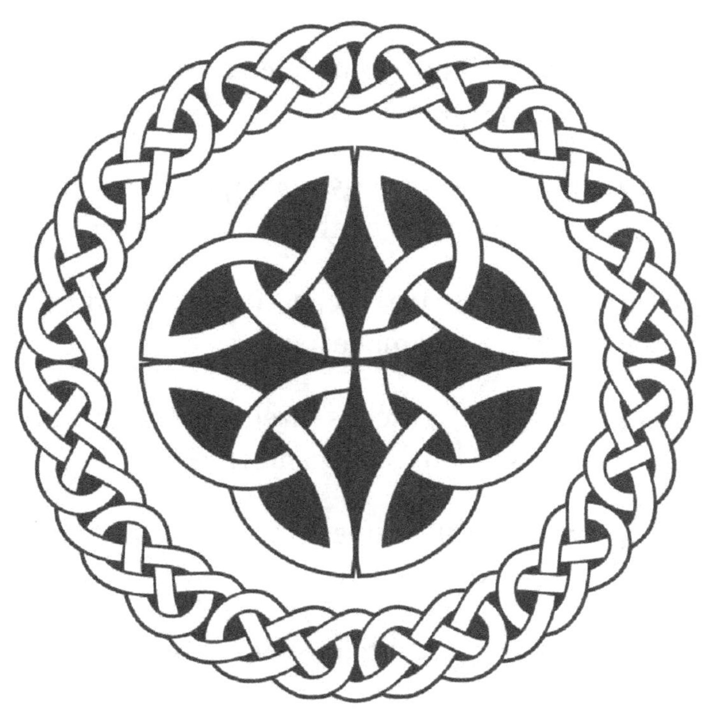

Required Materials

- Graph paper

- Compass

- Colored pencils

- An eraser

- Compass and protractor

Instructions

Follow these simple steps to create your own Celtic circles and squares.

Step 1: Divide your drawing paper into half and pick a particular point to be the circle's center.

Step 2: Measure two inches along the radius from the midpoint and make a mark.

Step 3: Make 1/4 inches three times apart that are moving back towards the center.

Step 4: Use your compass to set a point in the midpoint, to outside the mark.

Step 5: Draw your circle, keeping the point of the compass at the midpoint.

Step 6: Draw four such circles with the largest being 4" in diameter, the next being 3 1/2, 3, and 2 1/2, respectively.

Step 7: Use a protractor to line the 0 marks upon your center line and do the same on your midpoint center.

Step 8: Make little tick marks every 10 degrees. Ten degrees is about the same size as the 1/4" of a standard graph sheet.

Step 9: Use a ruler to draw in guidelines on both sides of the circle you've drawn. I know this is a lot, but you'll get the perfect Celtic Circle and square. Let's continue the process.

Step 10: Start drawing in the "bones" of the braid you've made.

Step 11: Draw in your curves & start the weaving pattern. Make sure you erase the bones before making your curves. Remember, your braid won't be a band of interlace when they connect if the number of curves on the outside edge can be equally divided by three.

Step 12: Draw two relatively long parallel lines that are 1/2 inches apart and make tic marks on the top and bottom every two inches.

Step 13: Draw in your top and bottom curves, ensuring they are centered between the tic marks and letting the right-hand side cross over the space onto the next arc as they will form the outer edge of your bands.

Step 14: Next, draw in the inner edge of your bands from the top and extend your lines a bit more to ensure that the inner edge is aligned to form the lower curved outer edge and create an "over" portion of the twist.

Step 15: Complete the lower curves while trying to keep the width of your bands even.

Don't worry if your first trial looks very messy. You've got an eraser, and you can always erase rough edges and pencil marks. Practice makes perfect. Once you keep practicing, your circle and square pattern will appear less messy.

Viking Animals

Hundreds of Viking jewelry items with various symbols are sold across different jewelry stores all over the world. Why are these Viking jewels famous? You may ask. There is no definite meaning and origin of these Viking symbols since most are anthropological, historical, and archaeological guesses. However, it is still necessary to understand the Viking symbols' true source, background, and meaning.

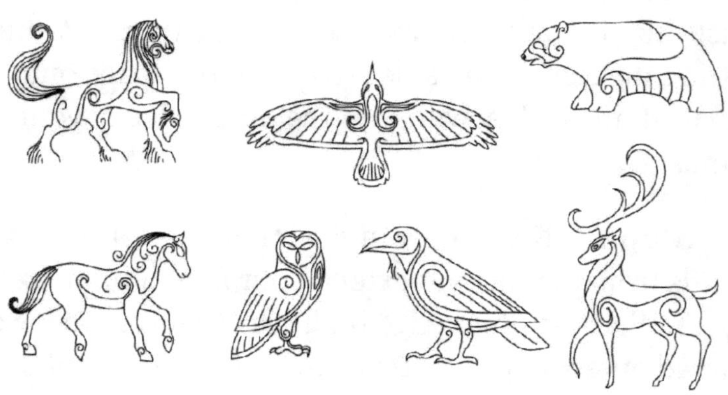

The Norse used these iconic Viking images and symbols during the Viking era. A high percentage of Modern Icelandic people have been argued to be direct descendants of Viking ancestors. A lot of these symbols such as the well-known Helm of Awe

(Icelandic: Ægishjálmur, Old Norse Œgishjalmr) and the Viking Compass (Icelandic: Vegvísir, for "signpost" or "Wayfinder") were said to have been found in ancient Icelandic books from the 16th century.

These books were a collection of old magical runes passed from one generation to another. However, some other Viking symbols have no proof of originating from the Viking era. An example is the Troll Cross, and the true origin of these symbols remains uncertain. At the end of the Viking era, Vikings were already beginning to blend with the other cultures they settled in. Many of the last few generations of these Vikings were often the children of Celtic, Slavic, English parents.

How to Draw a Viking Animal

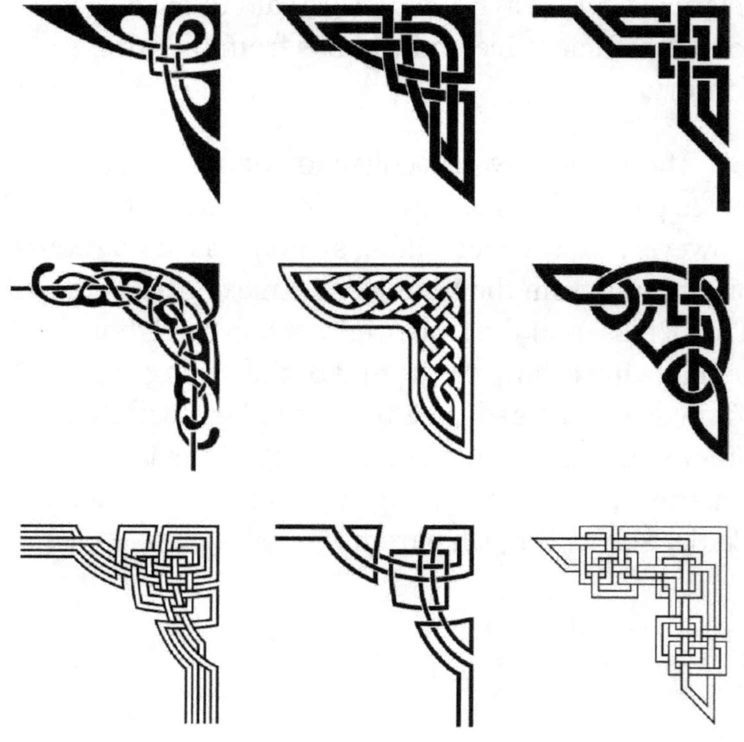

Step 1: Let's start by using a large oval shape to create the head of your Viking animal.

Step 2: Next, draw in a thin rectangle to represent the body, and you can also make the pants in the same pattern.

Step 3: Work repeatedly on this Viking animal by sketching the arms and the legs. No fingers are needed, so draw a simple circle to replace the fingers and shoes.

Step 4: Create the eyes and the pupils from large circles. Then draw smaller circular shapes to form the ears. The helmet is made using a rectangle with rounded corners while you create the horns from curved lines.

Step 5: Draw a few oval shapes to form the pupils while drawing a line representing the nose and mouth. Go ahead and draw a large beard around the mouth and some hair below the head.

Step 6: complete your Viking animal by adding a broad belt of the shirt and a pointed sword on the right hand of your drawn Viking animal.

Step 7: Add colors to make your Viking animal more aesthetic.

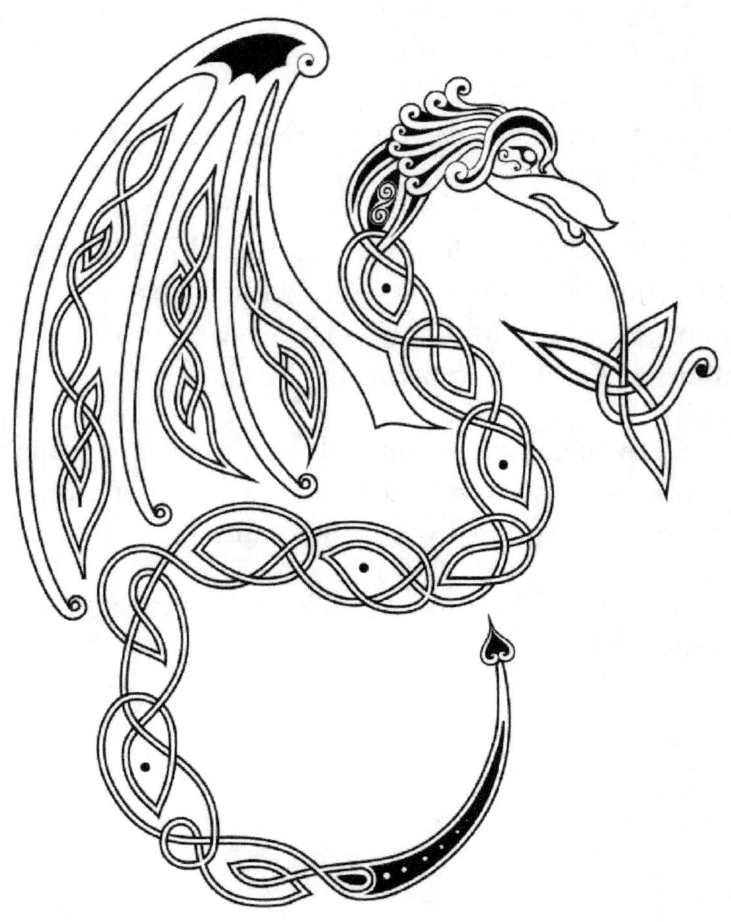

Celtic Religious Symbols and Their Meanings

Celtic symbols and signs have held incredible power for the ancient Celts in every way of life since a long time ago.

These ancient Celtic communities used Celtic symbols and images for worship, and they firmly believed in the power these symbols wielded. Now all of these have become a part of the Irish heritage and identity. Some of these Celtic symbols and their meaning includes:

- The Awen: The word 'Awen' first appeared in the 9th-century book titled "HistoriaBrittonum," which means inspiration or essence.

People attribute various meanings to the Celtic Awen symbol. One such interpretation is that the Awen represents the harmony of both opposites of the universe.

For instance, the two outer rays represent masculine and feminine energy, while the ray in the middle represents the balance between them.

- St. Brigid's Cross: St. Brigid's Cross is believed to be a Christian symbol, but ancient Irish Celtic Mythology associated Brigid's Cross with a life-giving goddess, known as Brigid of the Tuatha de Danann. When Christians came to settle in Ireland, the goddess became anglicized to St Brigid of Kildare. Most of her attributes, especially her association with fire, were transferred to the latter.

The cross is woven from rushes and straws and is used during the feast of Imbolc to signify the beginning of spring.

- Celtic Cross: Just like with the Brigid's Cross, many people associate the Celtic Cross with Christianity, although studies seem to suggest that this symbol predates Christianity by thousands of years.

The symbol has appeared in many ancient cultures, and according to one theory, the Celtic Cross represents the four cardinal directions of the earth. Another theory posits that the Celtic Cross represents the four essential elements, which are Earth, Air, Water, and fire.

The Celtic Cross has powerful representations and meanings that are a perfect reflection of the Celts' hopes and ambitions. While the Christians believe the Celtic Cross is undoubtedly a Christian symbol, research has proven otherwise as it has its roots in ancient pagan beliefs.

- The Green Man: The Green Man is represented in many cultures as the head of human-made foliage. This image is often seen in many buildings and structures in Ireland and even Britain. People believe the Green Man is a symbol of rebirth and the co-dependence and interconnectedness between nature and man.

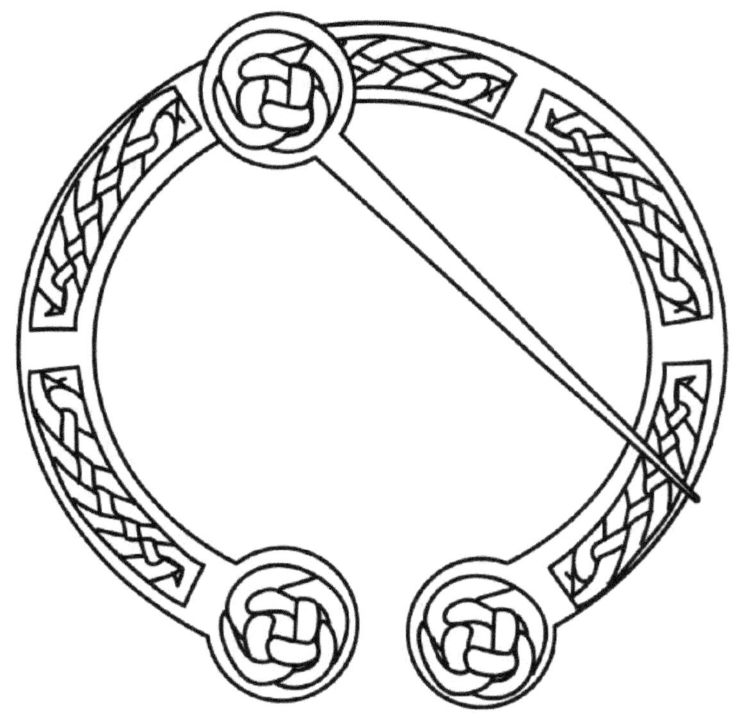

The Green man symbolizes the lushness of vegetation and also the arrival of spring and summer. Christian churches have also carved the Green man in their art, such as the Seven Green Men of Nicosia in Cyprus, a series of green men carved in the 29th century onto the facade of St Nicholas Church in Nicosia.

- The Tree of Life: The Celtic Tree of Life, also known as 'CrannBethadh' in Irish, are intricately interwoven branches and roots often associated with the Druids. It is a potent and earthy Celtic symbol. In representations, the branches reach for the sky, and the roots permeate the earth. For the ancient Celts, the Tree of Life represents balance and harmony.

It also symbolizes the close relationship between heaven and earth. It also stands for longevity, strength, and wisdom. The Celts also believed that the spirit of their dead ancestors lived in these trees.

They believed that these trees also symbolize rebirth (as they witnessed the trees shed old leaves during fall and grow new ones in spring), which made the tree highly revered. The unique thing about this symmetric Celtic is that when spun, its appearance always remains the same.

- Dara knot: The Dara Knot is one of the most popular Celtic symbols is the Dara Celtic Knot. This symbol is an interwoven design. It got its name from the Irish word 'Doire,' which means "oak tree." The Dara Knot symbol represents an ancient oak tree's root system and is made of intertwined lines with no beginning or end, which is common among Celtic Knot symbols.

There are several designs for the Dara Celtic Knot. However, all versions and modifications are centered on the oak tree's common theme and its roots. Ancient Celts and Druids revered nature, particularly old oak trees, and considered them sacred. They often saw the oak tree as a symbol of strength, power, wisdom, and endurance; hence the Dara Knot symbol represents inner strength, endurance, power, and wisdom.

Chapter Summary

- Celtic patterns are used for aesthetics and decorations.

- Celtic knots are widely used and represented in Christian monuments.

Were you able to create your own Celtic pattern?

In the next chapter, you will learn a few layout ideas.

Chapter Five: Layout Ideas

The Celtic layout can make or mar a Celtic art design. To a large extent, the layout determines the aesthetics of the knotwork. Remember that Celtic knot patterns are the combination of borders, corners, interlocking knots, and the designer's layout skills will determine how these things turn out. These borders, corners, and interlocking knots constitute the areas of concern when Celtic layout ideas are concerned.

Little wonder, designers, especially beginners in Celtic artwork, are eager to understand the fundamentals of Celtic borders, corners, interlocking knots, and all forms of dots and lines and how to use them to create amazing Celtic designs. This chapter will teach you two distinct methods of crafting unique and appealing layouts for your Celtic creations; tricks on how to create your own square, rectangle, or circular border, and some other incredible designs.

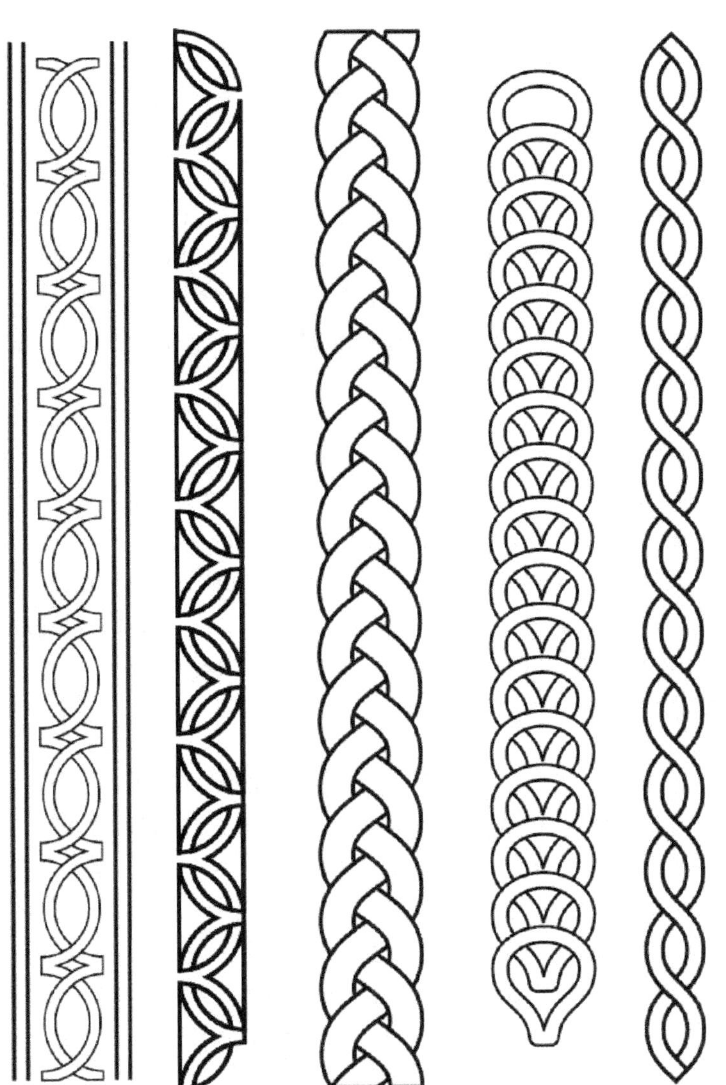

Layout Methods

Interlacing Without Erasing

There's nothing to erase when one uses this layout method. Dots used in creating the pattern are buried in the knotwork's background. So, at the end of the design, the background will be carved or painted, and there will be nothing to erase. Here is how to use this method.

Step 1: Sketch a few rectangular grids of dots. Fill up the section you want to add your knotwork but make sure that the dots are evenly spaced. To calculate the distance between dots, consider the width of the ribbons of your knotwork. Add a dot to the middle of each square to form a diagonal dot grid for the knotwork project.

Step 2: Add the breaks. Use breaks to vary the loop of your knotwork, or use the same pattern all through. The knotwork may run over lines, except the breaks. A break can join two or more lines vertically or horizontally. While a break could intersect a dot, one break must not cross another one within the design. Breaks can be used stylishly to create some striking effects in Celtic knotwork.

Step 3: Weave the ribbon. Locate the open area next to the break, and start the weaving from there. To indicate the start of the ribbon, sketch two diagonal lines in the center of two dots. Sketch two more diagonal lines opposite the first set and expand the drawing a bit to create a regular knotwork weaving pattern.

Step 4: Curve the breaks, but note that your ribbon must not cross your break. While your ribbon takes a diagonal slant, the breaks could be horizontal or vertical. So, just before you hit the break lines, find a way to bend your ribbon.

You don't need to create an initial layout before you can use this method. With the technique, all you need to put in place are the grids. Use this layout method to design great and amazing projects to amuse your friends and loved ones.

Centerline Knotwork

Most people prefer the first layout method. Why? They believe that the centerline knotwork is too complex to master. True, it is an ancient method of layout since it was used in the Book of Kells. With this method, you'll need to sketch more lines than expected and also erase some. Still, this layout method shares some similarities with the previous one. Here, I will show you the processes, and if it works perfectly for you, you can use it to design your knotwork layout.

Step 1: Sketch a few rectangular grids of dots. Yes, the first process is similar to that of the previous one. But, in this case, the number of dots in a direction should be odd. To make this happen, divide the odds in the direction by two, and you'll know if what you have is odd or not. Next, add a dot in the center of each square.

Step 2: Add the breaks. Control the ribbon with the break, just like you did with the first method. Still, you don't have to connect the dots. Center the break on the dots. Feel free to join the breaks if that will aid the aesthetics of your knotwork. Just remember that breaks cannot hit the dots directly. All you can use them to do is intersect two or more dots.

Step 3: Sketch the middle line. Connect your diagonal dots to create the ribbon's centerline. Follow this line until you need to avoid hitting the break. So, find a way to bend the middle line, but you can connect it with the nearest dot. Run the middle line till you get to where you initiated the drawing. Should you miss any dots, feel free to connect the dots again or initiate the process of sketching another centerline. So, as it stands, you'll have more drawings to sketch and more lines to erase.

Again, the centerline knotwork method is time-consuming. You'll have to create many centrelines and tilt them to your desired position to create your favorite pattern. Still, if you used a single line, you can easily modify your ribbon's movement just by altering your breaks. There's no way you can use the previous method to achieve this.

Step 4: Sketch the highway. Always consider your centerline as the road or pathway for your knotwork layout. Simply sketch the edges of the layout beside the centerline if you want the whole process to be very easy. Once this is done, you'll discover that your ribbon has three major lines— a center edge and two outer edges.

Step 5: Weave the ribbon. Identify two intersection points in the design. Consider them as the crossing points of the pathway of your knotwork. Use a few lines to bridge the two roads.

Step 6: Erase the centerline. Initially, I told you that this layout method uses lots of centerlines, and you'll need to erase a few ones after the whole design is done. So, take your time to erase the excess centerlines, one after the other.

Feel free to try these two layout methods to know the one that works best for you. The first method is considerably easier to use than the second one. Just know that the second layout method often leads to a more beautiful layout design.

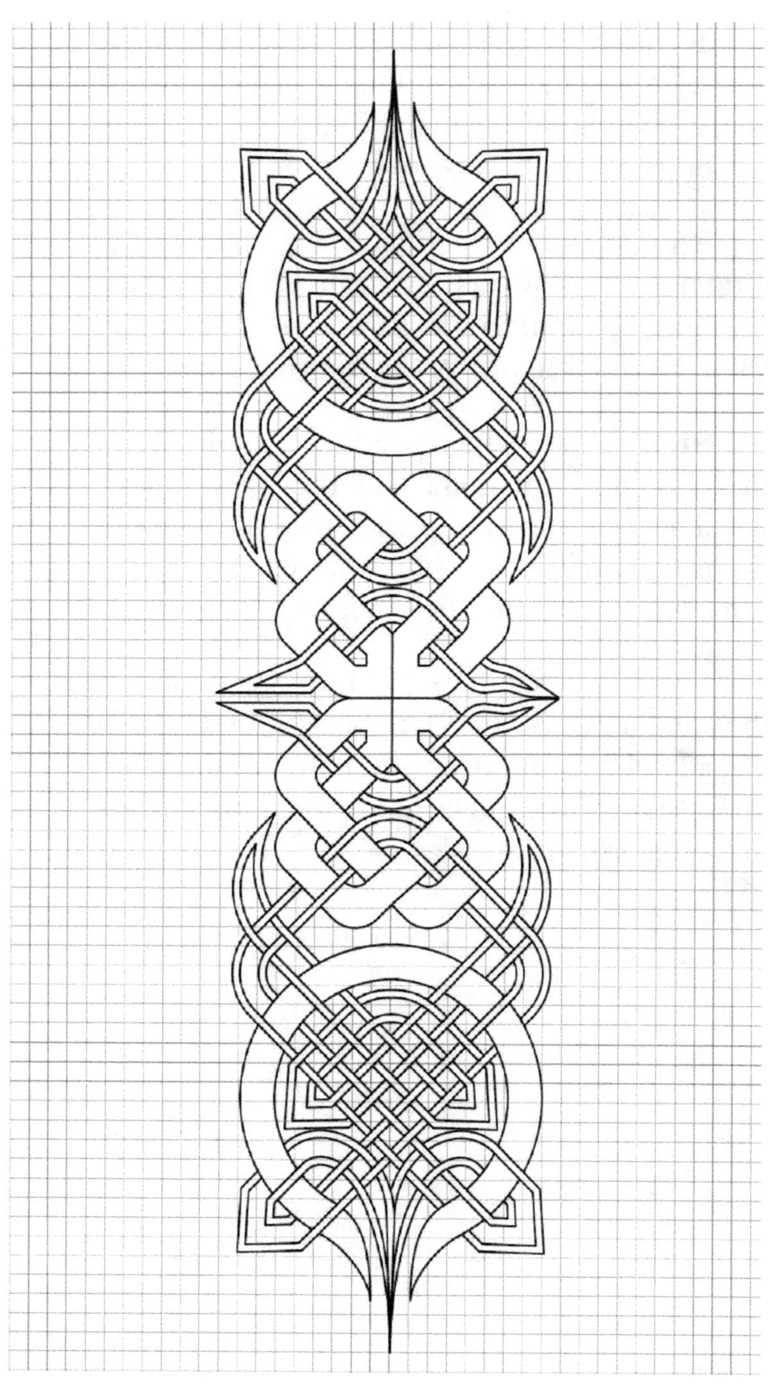

How to Create a Circular Border

A circular border is fair and fitting, but some people believe it is a bit complicated. Some say a circular border is easier than drawing straight lines. Fine. It depends on which one works best for you and how easy it is for you to create them. Still, both circular borders and straight lines can have a substantial visual impact on your Celtic knot. Here is how to design a circular border.

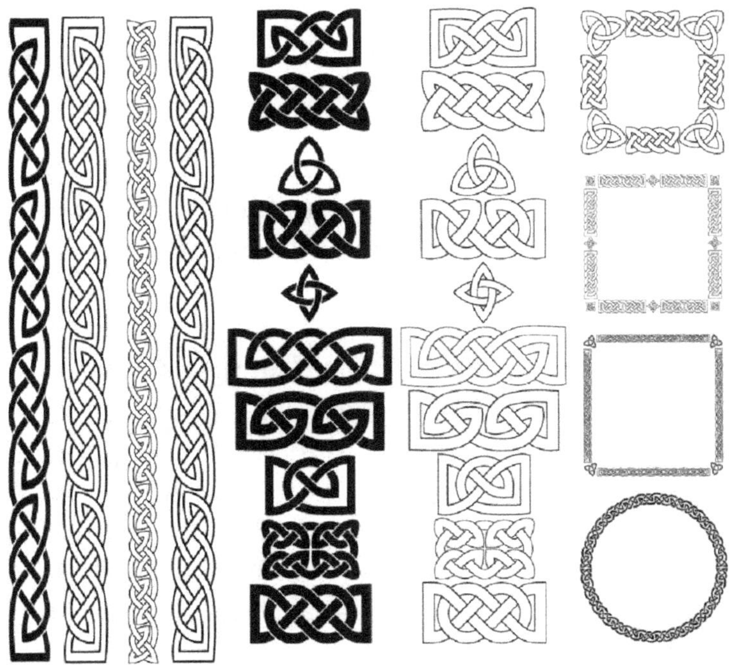

Required Materials

- Graph paper

- Colored pencils

- Compass and protractor

- An eraser

- Ruler

Instructions

Follow these simple steps to design your circular border.

Step 1: Divide your paper in half. Decide the point you intend to use as the middle of your circle. Measure 2 inches from the middle of the circle and mark the point.

Step 2: Sketch 3 additional marks from the middle of the circle, but keep them 1/4" apart. Position your compass to the circle's middle point and use your pencil to create a round shape.

Step 3: Sketch the circle. Create a circle from the middle point. Draw 4 circles— 4", 3 1/2", 3", and 2 1/2" respectively.

Step 4: Sketch your curves around the circle and add your weave pattern.

Step 5: Erase rough lines. Color your design. Feel free to use the color you want. Just make sure that you balance your color.

How to Design a Celtic Knot with a Rectangle Border

Borders aid the aesthetics of Celtic knots. They ensure that the designed knot looks attractive and appealing. Again, you can vary the rectangles, circles, and squares to create the knot you truly want. Good. Here is how to create a Celtic knot with a rectangle border.

Required Materials

- Grainy or graph paper

- Colored pencils

- An eraser

Instructions

Follow these simple steps to design a Celtic knot with a rectangle border.

Step 1: Use a grid to design the border. Just make sure that the grid is big, or you'll have issues perfecting this stage. Lay the grid on a flat surface and put the paper on it. Use your pencil to trace the grid to design your rectangle border.

Step 2: Finish the pattern. Stylishly work on the corners and glide your hand to the center of the knot. Here, you'll sketch two squares— one within the grid and the other one on the edges of the grid square. Add a few curves when you're connecting the squares if you want to make the design a little fancy. Sure, creativity is desirable here.

Step 3: Run the line over the grid a few times. Take your time here because you'll be going to run the line a couple of times again. Just make sure you get the shape you admire.

Step 4: Finish the design. Straighten and thicken the lines to make them look attractive and appealing. Feel free to color the design.

Creativity is key. Again, rather than creating four or five borders, stick to two. Create a frame and color the design. Use your favorite color.

Chapter Summary

- Celtic layout can be used to determine and aid the aesthetics of the Celtic knotwork.

- Borders, corners, and interlocking knots are used to create celtic layout.

In the next chapter, you will learn how to enhance your Celtic pattern with color.

Chapter Six:
A Guide to Enhancing Your Work with Color

Patterns are everywhere, and we must have seen and purchased different items with highly intricate colors and patterns. They are mostly aesthetic and best for decorations. However, you have to know how to create these patterns, especially as a designer. This is important because patterns invoke movement, aids color harmony, create visual texture, and make your work visually appealing.

What if I'm not into patterns? That is not a problem as many people feel that way until they create a pattern themselves. Creating a pattern can be quite tricky, especially for beginners, but you will become a professional at creating beautiful patterns with time. One predominant question here is this: How do you mix colors and patterns?

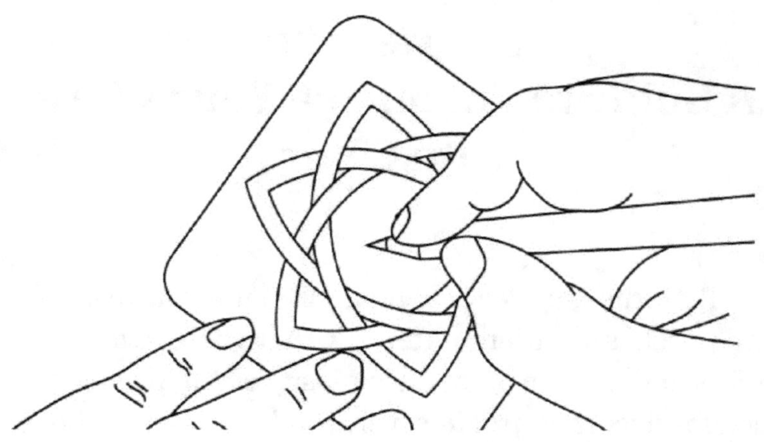

Know Your Colors

To create a perfect mix of colors and patterns, you have to outline your color scheme. You have to understand the 60-30-10 color rule. This means you have to choose three colors: the primary, secondary, and accent color in the 60:30:10 ratio, respectively. This will help you know which colors complement each other and how to incorporate these colors effectively.

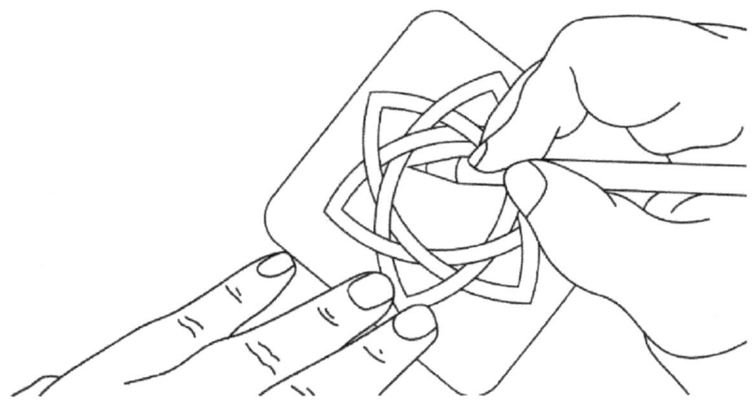

Your primary color (60%) is the most extensive color element and is often a neutral one. It is the color that anchors how the whole space would turn out. The secondary color (30%) is usually different from the primary color and creates a huge contrast to create a harmonious balance. Lastly, your accent color (10%) is mainly used for accessories and creates a huge visual impact.

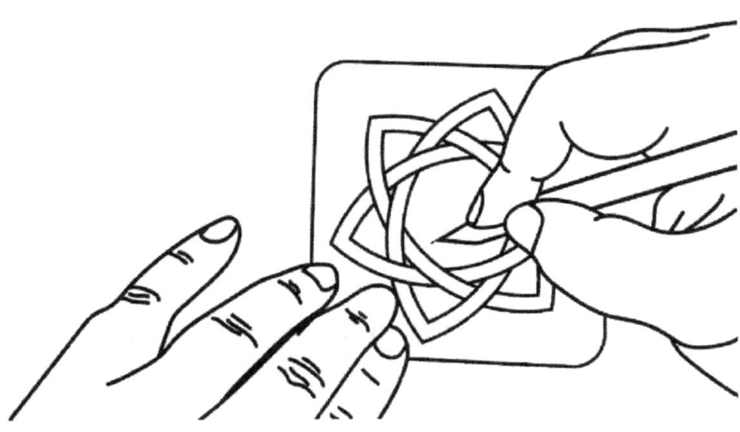

Know How to Balance the Color Temperature

Colors have temperatures, and these can either be warm or cool. Warm colors are red, yellow, and orange, while cool colors are blue, green, and violet. When choosing the right colors for mixing, choose both warm and cool to create a harmonious balance. Using only warm colors can create a visually stuffy effect, and using only cool makes your art appear visually chilly. However, a combination of both will make your art seem nice and appealing.

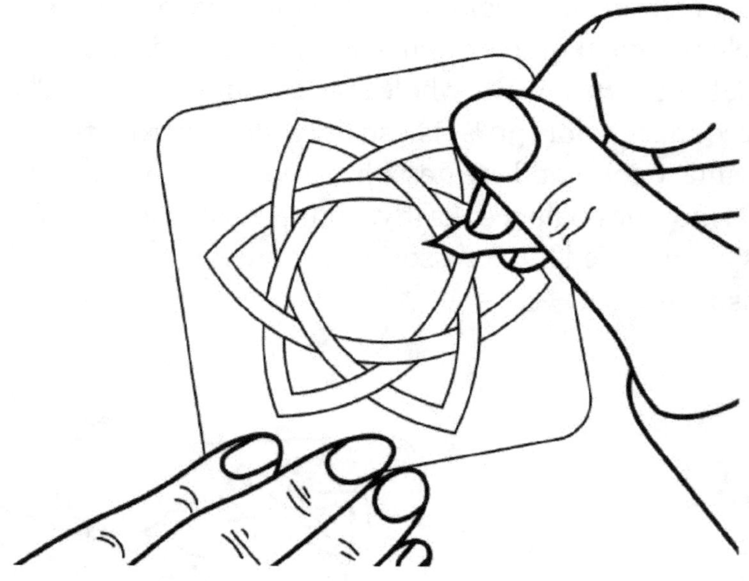

Use a Color Wheel

If you are still struggling with choosing the right colors, you should use an adjustable color wheel. Color wheels help you judge color undertones more accurately and also assist you in creating harmonious color combinations. They also help you know the difference between warm and cool colors.

You can use a color wheel to create vibrant color combinations as they help indicate what color pairings are harmonious. For example, all complementary colors are best for contrasting an accent, primary or secondary color. Also, a Triad (split complementary color) is best for selecting a 3-color limited pattern, while the Tetrad is used to choose an additional accent color for your art.

Gradient Colors Weaving with Rya Knots: Weaving Color

This topic is geared at teaching you how to weave a gradient color effect along with your soumak and plain weave, rya knots, and yarn. The main reason this is done is to create movement and depth in weaving and enhance the visuals.

Learning this technique is also great for creating transitions between textures of different yarns. All you have to do is add both colors alternatively to achieve this.

How to Weave Gradient Colors with Rya Knots

Rya knots are created with one, two, or more strands of yarn. When you see more colors on your Rya knot, it increases the color intensity of the knot. To weave gradient colors with Rya knots, there is a process of layering you have to follow.

Instructions

1. Get two yarns that are of different colors.

2. Pick two strands from each yarn.

3. Start weaving your first row with color.

4. Weave the second row with color 2.

5. Weave the first row again with color 1 and 2.

6. Weave the second row with color 1.

7. Start again by weaving the first row with color 1 and color 2.

Weave the second row with color 1 and color 2.

Repeat the process by weaving the first row with color 1.

Start the second row with just one strand of color 2.

Then create a third row with two strands of color 1.

There is another method to create a gradient color with Rya knots. The instructions are below:

Step 1: Weave a few rows of plain weave to serve as your base.

Step 2: Weave two or three rows of your Rya knot using color one.

Step 3: Always secure your knot after weaving two or three rows.

Step 4: After weaving a substantial amount of rows, use color two.

Step 5: Repeat the process alternatively depending on your desired outcome

Step 6: Make sure your knot has a combination of both colors, and always remember to secure your knots after weaving two to four rows.

Step 7: Introduce the third color you want to use.

Step 8: Repeat the process from step 6 to 1 in reverse order.

5 Simple Tips to Achieve Color Harmony In Your Oil Painting

What do you understand by the term 'Color Harmony'? The word itself is self-explanatory. Still, it has to do with combining colors in a way that is harmonious to the eyes. Most artists refer to it as the 'magical glue' connecting all elements of your painting together. When your colors lack harmony, even when you have a perfect idea, strong composition, and a powerful paint composition, you will still likely end up creating a painting that holds no appeal to the eyes that view them.

Colors are an essential part of our lives, and almost everything we see has color and is highlighted by the lighting conditions of the atmosphere. Natural colors often appear harmonious, and there is often a strong need to replicate these on your canvas. There are many rules as to how to achieve such harmony for complementary or analogous colors. You can reach the best color harmony when painting; only if you understand and practice the following tips, which we shall be discussing below.

1. Always start your painting with ground color. Doing this makes your work easier as you don't have to fill up every gap on your canvas. The ground color allows you to create a stable atmosphere that makes it easy to harmonize your painting. Your ground color can vary depending on what you want to paint.

2. Learn to use a limited palette. Buying every color feels good but using fewer colors, especially when mixing, has many benefits. Using too many colors can create an overall chaotic and disorganized effect. A limited palette makes it easier to mix, and it helps enhance color harmony.

3. One tricky tip to creating color harmony on your piece is to use different colors with the same painting brush. That is, don't wipe your brushes. When you do this, you'll discover that

although you used varying shades, they appear harmonious and share the same pigment.

4. Always add colors across your canvas for better blending and ensure that no area is untouched, which aids and adds to your piece's visuals. This helps to harmonize the colors and link all elements together.

5. Glazing your painting is a great way to achieve color harmony. Glaze your artwork to achieve a specific mood and reduce the intensity of the colors on the canvas. To add your glaze, use a retouching varnish or painting medium along with little paint to avoid cracks.

10 Oil Painting Techniques to Transform Your Artwork

Paintings are beautiful works of art, and as a painter, it is fun to paint lovely images and your imaginations on a canvas. However, you can go from painting simple crafts to creating a masterpiece using oil painting techniques.

Using the oil painting technique can be quite tricky as a beginner, and a mistake can ruin the result you are aiming for. Although there are several practical painting techniques to improve your painting art, it is still crucial that you know how you can also use oil painting techniques to help boost your painting skill and appearance.

If you want to give your art a boost with these professional oil painting techniques, you must note the ten fundamental tips for using the oil painting techniques available.

Hold Your Paint Brush Correctly

Many artists don't know this, but the way you handle your brush when painting, to some extent, determines how accurate your strokes will appear. Always hold your paintbrush at the end to gain maximum control of your strokes while painting. As an artist, it is essential to know how to handle your paintbrush to achieve fluidity and sensitivity when creating your strokes. You have to hold your paintbrush as far back as you can to achieve this.

As a beginner who is still learning to paint, this may prove a bit uncomfortable, but with constant practice, you will discover that it gives you some measure of control as you can paint with your whole arm, rather than using just your wrist, which gets tiring after a while.

Master Your Brush Orientation

Knowing your brush orientation is a great way to produce professional paintings. You don't always have to use only the flat side of your brush, as every paintbrush has two orientations and sides. Learn to use every angle of your brush as you get to create sharper lines, strokes, and control how these appear on your canvas. Once you understand this, you will discover that you become faster and more versatile when painting.

Vary Your Pressure

The pressure you apply when painting, especially when creating your lines and strokes, determines if that painting will come out perfect or messy. Avoid using a lot of pressure when handling your paintbrush, as the less pressure you apply, the better the texture of the painting. There are different types of strokes, and these are the Light, Medium, and Heavy strokes. Get acquainted with these strokes and the right pressure to apply to create each of them and achieve the desired effect.

Vary your pressure appropriately to ensure that they match your strokes for an overall aesthetic effect as the more massive your pressure, the more your paints will create ridges along the sides of your brushstrokes.

Harness the Power of the Painting Medium

As an artist, the best way to control paint is to use a painting medium. The painting medium can help modify your paints in ways you can't imagine. A painting medium is a mixture of solvent and oil that is used to control your paint. When you add a lot of painting medium to your regular paint, it becomes transparent and flat. Meanwhile, adding just a little painting medium makes your paint thicker, giving it a mayonnaise-like effect.

Keep Your Color Pure

Owning different paint brushes is essential. Keeping them clean is also another important task. Using a messy paint brush can mess up the color you want to use for a particular painting. Therefore, you have to keep your brushes clean after every painting session to ensure that they preserve the intensity of the colors you want to use for a new painting.

Use Two-Color Mixtures If You Can.

One trick to achieving a vibrant painting is to use as little color mix as possible. Using too many color mix can make your artwork appear dull and less intense. Instead, choose only two colors and mix them with white. You'll discover that your painting comes out better, and you become more efficient at selecting the right colors and how to combine them properly.

Learn Not to Over-Mix

Learn only to mix as much as is necessary for the painting you are working on. When combining colors, mix them as necessary before applying your strokes and lines. When you over-mix colors, your painting becomes a messy pile of uninteresting and inconsistent paint. When you mix correctly, you create a vivid and aesthetically pleasing artwork.

Use As Much Paint As You Desire

Use as much paint as you desire to achieve the perfect painting. Do not hold back on achieving your desired result because you are trying to save up some paints. There are times when you don't require heavy painting. However, certain paintings require heavy strokes, so you have to use enough paint to achieve that. Don't swirl your brush over a thin pool of paint on your palette. Use as much paint as necessary to create a perfect piece.

Use Wet Versus Dry Brush

You need to remember that you can always paint directly on a wet surface and allow it dry, then use damp paint on it again. That way, your color will blend smoothly on the canvas, which is best for getting gradients and transitions. On the other hand, using a dry brush will give your painting a more textural effect, ideal for painting dirt or brick.

Use the Palette Knife

The palette knife isn't only for mixing paint. You can use this tool to create exciting paint strokes on your canvas. Sometimes, you don't always need a paintbrush to create the perfect. Using a palette knife is best for creating unpredictable and textural strokes when painting, which might be challenging to achieve if you use a paintbrush.

Chapter Summary

- Celtic patterns are used to decorate many items such as pendants, necklaces, and rings.

- Carefully balance your color to enhance the aesthetic of your Celtic knotwork

In the next chapter, you will learn line enhancements. See you there!

Chapter Seven: Line Enhancements

Line enhancement is a unique element in design that accelerates and improves the interface for the users. This doesn't indicate that you have to use this technique for task completion, but it is a method to quicken the design process. Users apply enhancement methods to accelerate their design. It is also referred to as an accelerator or shortcut. There are many ways of enhancing lines in the design. You will learn those methods in this chapter.

How to Add Accents and Symbols

There are many accented letters and symbols available to be included and not limited to l é, ñ, à, ó. The simple way to add emphasis is to use only those symbols that are important to your design. These symbols help to enrich your design. There are two methods of adding accented symbols. You can add it through Adobe Glyphs palette or keyboard shortcuts. I will teach the two methods to add accent and symbol from the comfort of your home.

Add accents and symbols through Adobe Glyphs' palette.

Required Materials

- Computer system

- Adobe InDesign software

Instructions

Follow these simple steps to add your accent and symbols through Adobe Glyphs' palette.

Step 1: Install Adobe InDesign software on your personal computer.

Step 2: Click on Document in Adobe InDesign, then select letter.

Step 3: Select Windows, after you will click on Type and Tables, then open new Glyphs. The Glyphs palette will assist you in getting all the characters available for the font of your choice.

Step 4: Click the glyph you want two times and use it.

Step 5: To add the glyph, right-click on the mouse and choose Add to Glyph Set, then attach your desired glyph.

How to Add Symbol through Keyboard Shortcuts

Materials needed

- Computer system

- InDesign software

- Keyboard

Instructions

Follow these simple steps to add accent and symbol through keyboard shortcuts

Step 1: Click on your InDesign software.

Step 2: Open a new document.

Step 3: Use different shortcuts to input your desired accents and symbols. For instance, to input LowerCase Acute Accent, you will click on ALT+E and instantaneously press the letter A or another vowel you desire on your keyboard. For Upper Case Acute Accent, you will Click on ALT+E, and immediately you will tap SHIFT+A or another vowel of your desire.

How to Add Language Accent Characters

This is one of the most difficult tasks to accomplish, especially for those who use computers. You might find it difficult to modify the accent and character. You will learn step by step methods of adding the language accent character. The Language Accent software can allow for easy addition of these characters and at the same time help you to learn the keyboard shortcuts associated with that character.

Instructions

Follow these simple steps to insert your language accent tool.

Step 1: Turn on the Language Accent tool. You can achieve this by clicking on settings on your InDesign tool. You will see and turn on the Language Accents and other tools to intermediate the design and make it simple.

Step 2: Interface. After turning on your language accent tool, a new language accents button will appear at the down part in the Design Tools sidebar. Click this button to open the Language Accents controls. After clicking on the button, an instruction will pop up.

Using Language Accent Tool to Create Content

After turning on your language accent character tool, you will have to create content with it. Although it may look cumbersome at first, practice from time to time will simplify it. I will teach you this method today.

Instructions

Step 1: Open your design software, click on the editing page, and then press Launch Design Tools.

Step 2: when you get to the Design Tools menu, press the Language Accents button.

Step 3: Choose the language of choice from the pop-up list.

Step 4: Move the mouse cursor to the part where you would like to input an accent character.

Step 5: Tap the button two times for the accent you would like to add.

Step 6: Then, you press the Save button.

The decoration is an essential part of interior design. Decorating with pattern will help you lift your home's face from ordinary to extraordinary and make it look attractive. You can add this pattern to an interior scheme such as the wallpaper, curtains, tiles, and bed linen. Decorating with the use of pattern most times looks like a Herculean task. The actual truth is that if you follow the simple rules, you will be able to add a bold design to your home with confidence.

Floral Pattern

This is a Flower-base design. This design is old fashioned, but it is evergreen. The floral design is suitable for everyone, including those who love a more subtle, abstract floral motif.

Balance

The main essence of adopting a pattern in your home is to achieve balance. You can accomplish this by spreading the design in your room. Concentrating on the pattern in a spot will make it look drab and not attractive. A combination of block colors that go in line with the color available in your design will help achieve the balance. Also, the size of your room determines the type of design or pattern you will use.

A large room should be used for a large design while a small room will be perfect for a small design.

When you are choosing stripes, select the ones that match your room. For instance, a room with greater height will be matched by vertical lines, while a wide room will be attractive with horizontal lines.

Mixed patterns

Mixing patterns create a better impression in the house. Although, using too much color may not make the room look mature. To mix color, you need to experiment with the pattern you have selected. For instance, if you are using floral patterns, try to combine large scale prints with tiny foliage designs. Whichever design you choose, you must include some white and complementary colors into the mix. This will have a total effect on your design.

Geometric

Repetition is the secret tool that makes geometric patterns attractive and exotic. The gorgeous look of the pattern makes us feel safe and content. Another way round, if you fall into a square design, change it with curvy ceramics, soft linens, and organic shapes such as pot plants.

Where Can I Use Patterns?

Patterns can be used in a variety of ways in the living room. It can be used to beautify your soft furniture such as cushions, rugs, and major furniture items such as a sideboard, coffee table, or sofa. This is to reduce the number of designs to a sizable one and balance them with standard colors. For instance, in the bedroom, a designed bed cover can be a decision point to a plain room when used hand in hand with straight colors in sheets and blankets.

A designed tile on the floor can change a utilitarian area into a decorative and beautiful one in the bathroom. The same goes for the kitchen. A well-patterned tile in a plain kitchen can make it look mature and add some personality. When you pick a designed tile for your kitchen or bathroom, make sure you repeat the same color from the pattern in some areas to achieve balance. This may be added through curtains, storage baskets, or towels in the bathroom.

Tropical

This is all about establishing a sense by bush or forest. This design makes it look as if you are going to town with numerous designs with plant imprints. Adding this to the wall brings a sense of beauty and maturity. Include tropical artwork to improve the face of your room. You must have it at the back of your mind that you must not stress your eye by applying too many colors. Instead, use a simple and balanced color for contrast.

Wallpaper

Using wallpaper is another good way to add design to your living space. There are many awesome wallpapers you can choose from out there. Animal prints, forest print, cities, and nature are significant wallpapers used for making a tropical feeling in your living space. However, your budget must also suit every decoration style you choose.

Also, your living space's size should determine the type of wallpaper you are going to select. For instance, a small space should consider ornate wallpaper. Also, placing a paper alcove at the back of shelves or under the kitchen island should be considered. Note that choosing an attractive wallpaper will make your room and other living space a joy to behold.

How to Use Background Patterns in Interior Design

The design placed on your walls, ceilings, and floors can make a special background effect for the room. It will interest you to know that a good background interior design can ameliorate bad architecture design, such as using a vertical stripe to push up the low ceiling and amend lack of a view by choosing a mural. Sometimes you can add or texture to sheetrock walls. However, there is a need to follow the step by step methods to using pattern as a background.

Step 1: Select a design and its color in accordance with the size of the room. To choose the most practical design and color for your room, always have your room's size in the back of your mind.

For small rooms, you should choose a simple colored design with soft backgrounds. For Medium rooms, you can select strong colored designs with simple backgrounds to make the room look spacious, and for the large rooms, pick a strong and serious design with interesting background colors.

Step 2: Pick a design according to its compatibility with the size of the house's style. Try and avoid an old design for a Modern structure. Also, you must consider the basic architectural patterns of your house and your area if available. However, for contemporary rooms, you should use geometric designs with no colors. For old rooms, pick a traditional design, especially those that are based on a historical event.

Step 3: Measure the size of your design to the room size. Make use of small designs in small rooms, normal designs in medium rooms, and large-scale designs in spacious rooms.

Design Rules for Textures and Patterns

Texture and pattern are subtle elements to use. What you can see and touch are very important, so it forms an essential design element. While patterning a room, you should add those elements that improve your experience of space.

Tips on How to Use Texture and Pattern in Your Home

1. Don't downplay the influence of texture and pattern.Both elements are capable of making your room look attractive.

2. You should use textures and patterns to create enough space for a particular purpose or an individual.

3. Use a direct light to improve the quality of the texture.

4. Be careful with how you use high-contrast patterns. It may be disorientating, so use them subtly in your interior.

5. Pick your wallpapers and fabrics with a vertical pattern and then lay more emphasis to allow a better impression of the height.

6. Non-geometric wallpaper may help to create a pseudo effect on the wall when irregularities appear.

7. High designs may attract the attention of the observer towards the pattern, and it is powerful.

8. Select a texture and design to create areas of interest to guide the eye to particular focal points.

Chapter Summary

- Line enhancement improves the aesthetics of Celtic knotworks.

- Creativity and patience are desirable traits for every aspiring Celtic art designer.

In the next chapter, you will learn how to create a Celtic knot decoration.

Chapter Eight:
Create a Celtic Knot Decoration

Celtic designs are beautiful and appealing. People use knots to design their necklaces, jewelry, and fabrics. Come to think of it, the fantastic beauty of Celtic knots is possible because of the stylish pattern of its decoration. Still, nothing but your creativity determines the beauty and attraction of your Celtic knot. Just pay keen attention to how you design your Celtic knot to make it charming and adorable. In this chapter, I will teach you how to create a foldable Celtic knot embellishment.

How to Create a Loop Square

Call it a loop or diamond square, and you're on point. The loop square is beautiful and attractive. Use it to create a striking effect in your home, and you'll love it. How you place the design matters, and you'll need to up your creativity a little bit to make it look perfect. The loop square isn't hard to create. You can do it right there in your home. How? Here is how.

Required Materials

- A pair of scissors

- Glue

- An aluminum finish paper

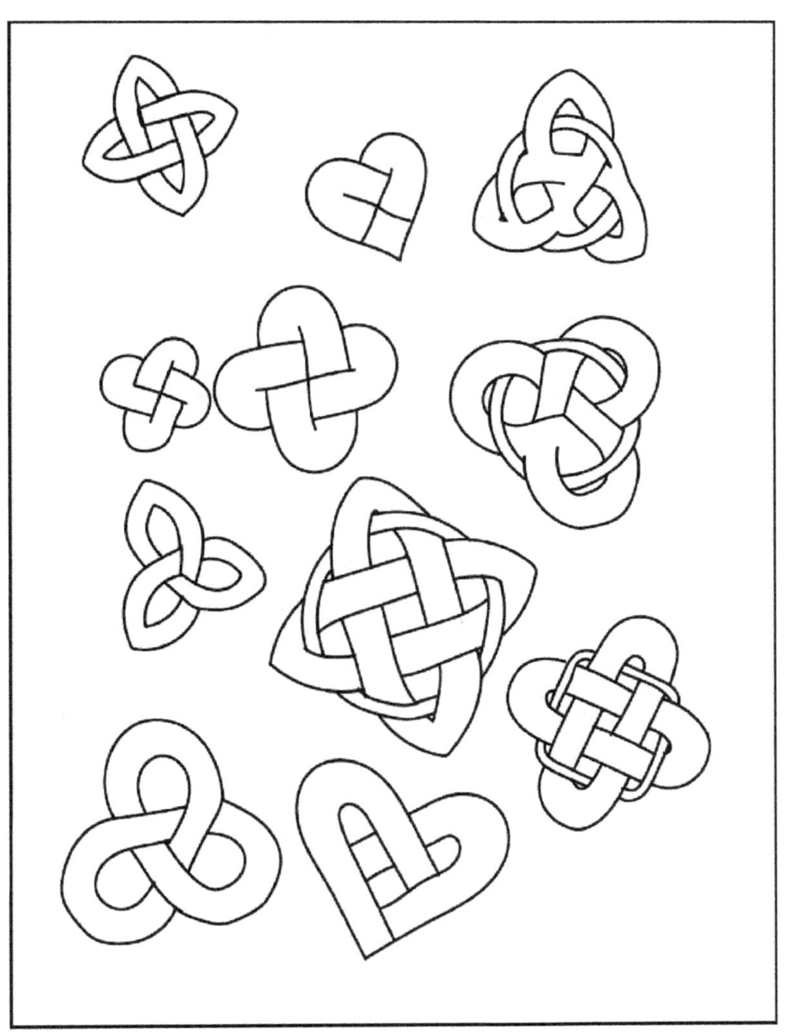

Instructions

Follow these simple steps to create your loop square.

Step 1: Trim your paper a bit and shape each paper's arm to form the base.

Step 2: Fold the arm to back, front, or center, depending on how you want it to look.

Step 3: Swing back the end of each loop and position the center loop in the front of your knot.

Step 4: Raise the arm over the loop and glue ends with the arm.

Crefoil, that's the name of the Celtic knot shape you just designed.

How to Design a Tote Bag

I love Tote bags because they are beautiful and attractive. These colored bags are thrilling, and they are perfect for your loved ones. You can surely design your own Tote bag in the comfort of your home. I will lead you through the process. Here's how to design the bag.

Required Materials

- Two pieces of fabric (vary the color)

- Sewing machine

- Needle

- Thread (according to Needle)

- A pair of scissors

Instructions

Follow these simple steps to design your own Tote bag.

Step 1: Create a body for the Tote bag. Sew the right sides of the fabric together. Stitch the top of the fabrics before you join the seams.

Step 2: Ready two pieces of color-blocked rectangles, cut them into 15" by 17" strips, and join them to the 3 sides of the sewn fabric.

Step 3: Design the lining. Just make sure the lining is a little bit smaller than the exterior part of the bag.

Step 4: Match the corners of the bags while they attach the wrong side of one fabric to the other. Fold the corners to align the bottom and side seam. Watch as a triangle is formed.

Step 5: Leave a few inches above the triangle and stitch on a straight line to create another corner. Hide the corner seam by flipping out the exterior part of the bag.

Step 6: Press the top of the bag a little bit and stitch the interior edge. Cut excess fabric and thread.

How to Design a Celtic Knot with Dots

Dots are great design options for Celtic knots. Creating dots and joining them to design Celtic knots is fun and interesting. Using a few dots to design a Celtic knot will be interesting and worthwhile, although the process may look a little bit complicated. Sure, you can master it and use dots to design a Celtic knot right there in your home. How can I do it? No worries. Here's how.

Required Materials

- Graph paper

- Colored pencils

- Ruler

- An eraser

Instructions

Follow these simple steps to design your own Celtic knot with dots.

Step 1: Sketch a few rectangles of dots. Create even dots on one side of the rectangle while the other side should have odd dots.

Step 2: Locate the diagonal lines pointing to one direction, fill them appropriately, and sketch a few diagonal lines in the other direction facing the previous lines.

Step 3: Join the lines across the walls and those along the corners.

Step 4: Color the spaces within the lines. Feel free you use your favorite colors. Use thick or thin lines to create your Celtic knot.

Step 5: Add extra lines and edges to beautify the knot. Just join the horizontal or vertical dots to create additional edges and lines to spice up the Celtic knot.

Step 6: Erase extra lines and edges.

Artists continue to be inspired to create Celtic knots because of its many lovely designs and iterations. In Celtic mythology, knots symbolize the sacredness of the universe and the elements that hold life firmly. Key and step patterns, including spirals, are tied in a continuous stylized rope, unlike knots' graphical sketches. Again, Celtic knots vary from one another in the areas of complexity and shape, and you might have seen them in ancient manuscripts, local Irish pubs, and tattooed bikers. Sure, these knots add no small beauty to items they embellish. In our robust interactions with established modern Celtic knot designers, we learned a few tricks and twists in the meaning, history, and how to create Celtic knots using Adobe illustrator. Here, I will run through the whole process to easily use these knots for decoration purposes.

Designing a Celtic Knot

Alexander Babich is the manager of MacoshDesign. He confessed that the animated film he watched aided his interest in Celtic knots—the major character stylishly designed amazing Celtic patterns and designs in the film, which enchanted Alexander. So, as time went by, Alexander studied. He studied Celtic designs extensively and later created his personal Celtic designs. He sees the whole thing as solving a crossword and creating something unique and extraordinary. An intricate knot turns out great if you carefully and creatively interlace your strips. For Alexander, place one strip over the loop and another one below it. Find a way to twist the knot and carefully connect the two ends of the strip to attain one infinite line. He called this the magic of Celtic knot design. Here is Alexander's process of creating a Celtic knot.

- Design your backdrop grid: Use your Adobe illustrator to design a vertical A4 document. Click the art board and select 'Rectangular Grid Tool Options.' Change grid weight to 0.1mm while the stroke color remains 0.255.255. Click the illustrator menu to move stroke units from General to millimeters, if it is not already there by default. Use the 'Direction Selection Tool' to create a few vertical and horizontal lines before you push the weight up slightly, from 0.1mm to 0.25mm.

Change the weight of the grid's outer line to 0.35mm. To select the grid, click Selection Tool> Object> Transform> Move and alter the parameters. Get a few copies of the grid. Next, click Selection. Then, Tool> Object> Transform> Move to change the

parameters again. Use these settings to arrive at a 5"
by 5" squares grid.

- Horizontal: 0

- Vertical: 10

- Distance: 10

Click Object> Group to group the squares you are
using to create the outline. Save the grid because you
can use it to design your favorite Celtic pattern and
ornament.

- Adjust the backdrop grid: Sure, you'll need to
  adjust your grid for every ornament you plan to
  design, especially if you're using the same grid
  for your Celtic projects. Just highlight the grid,
  select all, and copy the grid. Use these setting
  parameters.

- Horizontal: 50mm

- Vertical: 0mm

Copy the grid twice to have 4 copies. You can
press Ctrl+D to execute this action. Also, click 'Ellipse
Tool' and locate the intersection of the first horizontal
line and the second vertical line. Sketch your circle
from the intersection point and set width and height
to 40 mm. Highlight the circle. Use Ctrl+Shift+M to
copy it six times to arrive at eight circles. Be guided

with the circle if you want to create excellent symmetrical Celtic knots.

- Use your hand to draw the Celtic knot ornament. Start with a few sketches. Just remember that you can't have a perfect drawing. And, what you call imperfections could enhance the aesthetics of your design. Personally, I don't fancy the idea of drawing with a regular pencil. Most times, what you have is just like the ink shade. So, I think a blue pencil is better, although the final decision rests on your shoulders. Again, since Adobe Illustrator can differentiate between drawing with a blue pencil and the regular black ink, you don't need to erase anything before the software can trace your design.

Feel free to do a rough drawing to master the knot you intend to design. Make the drawing accurate as soon as you get the shape you are looking for. Start, center, and end are the three distinct elements of the design. So, endeavor to get it right from scratch, or there will be some issues at the end of the Celtic design. Still, you need to alternate the stripe. Line it top-down to create a striking effect. Also, pay keen attention to the grid when you're dealing with this step. Depending on your color preference, you can use two colors of pens to perfect this stage. To further advance the striking effect, add a few curves and width to your designed stripe.

Use a thin technical pen to trace the knot's edges and a thicker one to perfect the whole drawing. But, if you are confident and composed, use only the thick pen. Scan the drawing or move it to your Adobe libraries through Adobe Capture.

- Use Vector to create a seamless Celtic knot border: Open an Adobe Illustrator document and drag your drawing into the page. Click Image Trace and choose the Black and White tracing style. Feel free to use the settings above. Just make sure that you mark the box close to 'Ignore White' and unmark the one beside 'Strokes.' Next, change the tracing to paths. How? Open the control panel and click 'Expand.' Another way to do this is: click control panel > Object > Image > Expand. Great! Click the Line Segment Tool to sketch two vertical lines. Station the lines in the three elements I already talked about—start, middle, and end elements.

Click the Pathfinder panel to use the options there to enhance your drawing. You can also use Shift+Ctrl+F9 to run this process. Mark the box beside 'Divide and Outline Will Remove Unpainted Artwork' and click 'Ok.' Remember to click 'Divide' in the panel. Ungroup these elements by pressing Shift+Ctrl+G. The Celtic knot is ready but let's add a few details to make it charming and attractive.

- Add details. Just alter the fill to add a few vertical and outline lines. Go through the connection points to select the background you want and scale it up a bit to differentiate thin lines from thick ones. Why? The pattern has to be very clear for people to love it. Copy and print the pattern once you finish designing it. Adopt this pattern for your multiple designs. You could vary your designs by creating a few ropes, enhancing the background with more decorations, initiating shading, or simply by adding a few strokes. However, try to avoid a situation where all the knot's vertical lines connect. Also, a perfect drawing does not exist. What you call imperfections may breathe life on the Celtic knot. Be creative with your decorations so that you can end up with an appealing and colorful Celtic pattern.

Chapter Summary

- Celtic designs are bold and beautiful, and they are used to design necklaces, jewelry, and other fabrics.

- You need to up the level of your creativity to create one.

In the next chapter, you will learn more about Celtic knotted coasters.

Chapter Nine:
Celtic Pattern Knotted Coasters

Have a little more yarn left? These coasters are the best way to put those bits and pieces to use. These knots are handy, and the beautiful thing is that they are easy and fun to create.

Carrick Bend Mat Knot

The Carrick bend mat is also known as the thump mat or the more popular Carrick mat. It is a classic Turk's head weave and is related to the Turk's head knot. A Carrick bend-mat knot holds a significant value in some religions due to its interwoven structure.

People use the Carrick bend-knot pattern to create an aesthetically pleasing design on table mats or hot pads. The true Carrick bend is referred to as the full or double Carrick bend because of the eight crossings where each strand of rope passes over and under alternatively.

There are two types of Carrick Bend knots.

1. Single Carrick bend: these are less secure knots, and some examples are the granny, thief and reef knot, the sheet bend, among others.

2. Double Coin Knot: here, the tag end comes out
    of the same side instead of emerging diagonally.

To create a Kringle mat, follow these steps.

Step 1: Use a 10" cotton cord when making your
Kringle mat. Find the middle of the cord.

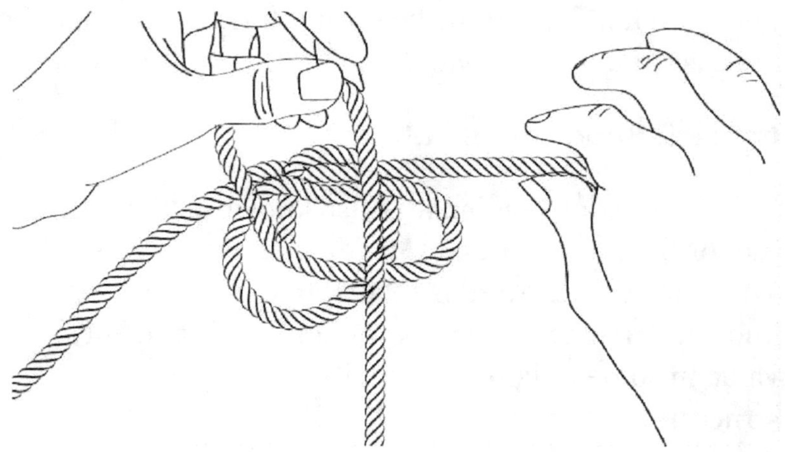

Step 2: Bring the cord's right end over the left
and vice versa over three strands. Bring the right end
under, then over, and under alternatively, and also
make the left end go under, over, and under in the
same manner.

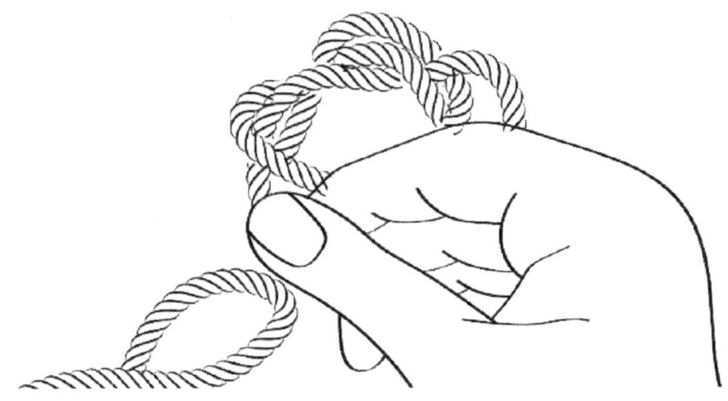

Step 3: Once you have done that, your mat base is set. You could double or trip this by making each end parallel till your knot is complete.

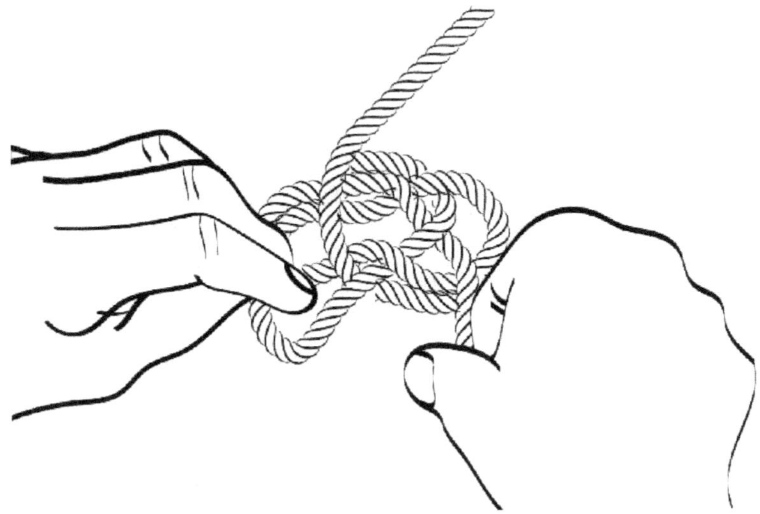

Step 4: Trim off the rough edges.

To make your Carrick bend-mat knot, you can follow these steps.

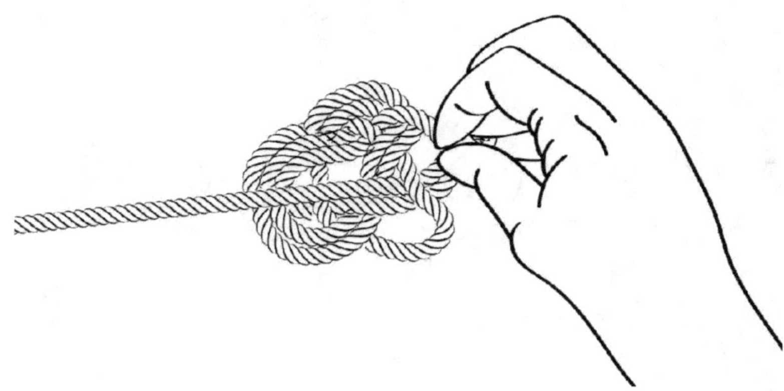

Step 1: Use a 10" out of the cotton cord.

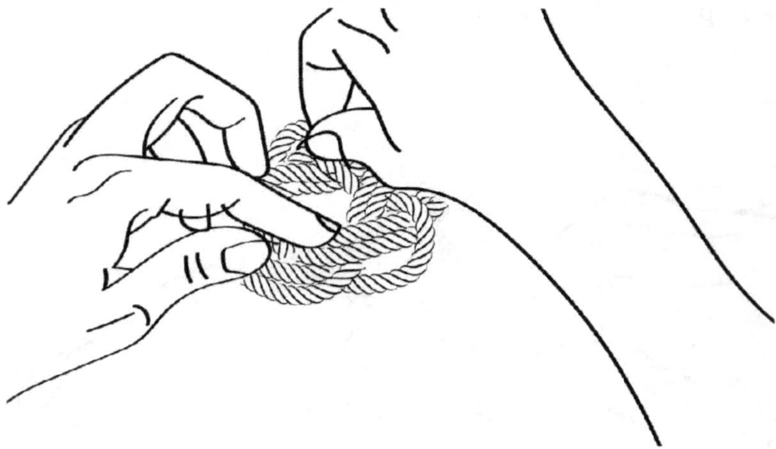

Step 2: Middle the cord and set the right end over the left to create a loop. Continue going over the two strands of the loop you just made, under the left-hand end. Once that is done, your mat base is complete.

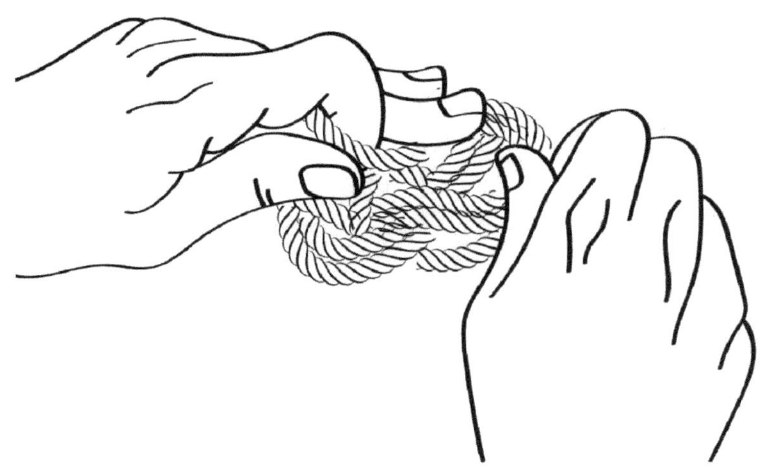

Step 3: Take each end, go parallel to the appropriate strand, tie each strand with a constrictor knot, and trim off any rough edge.

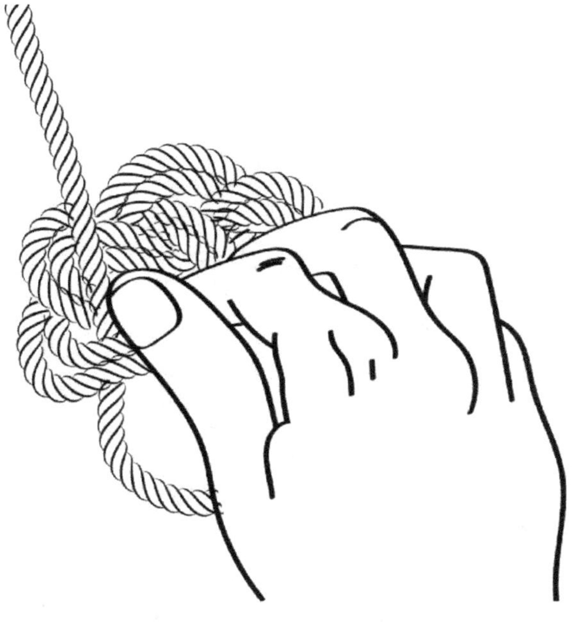

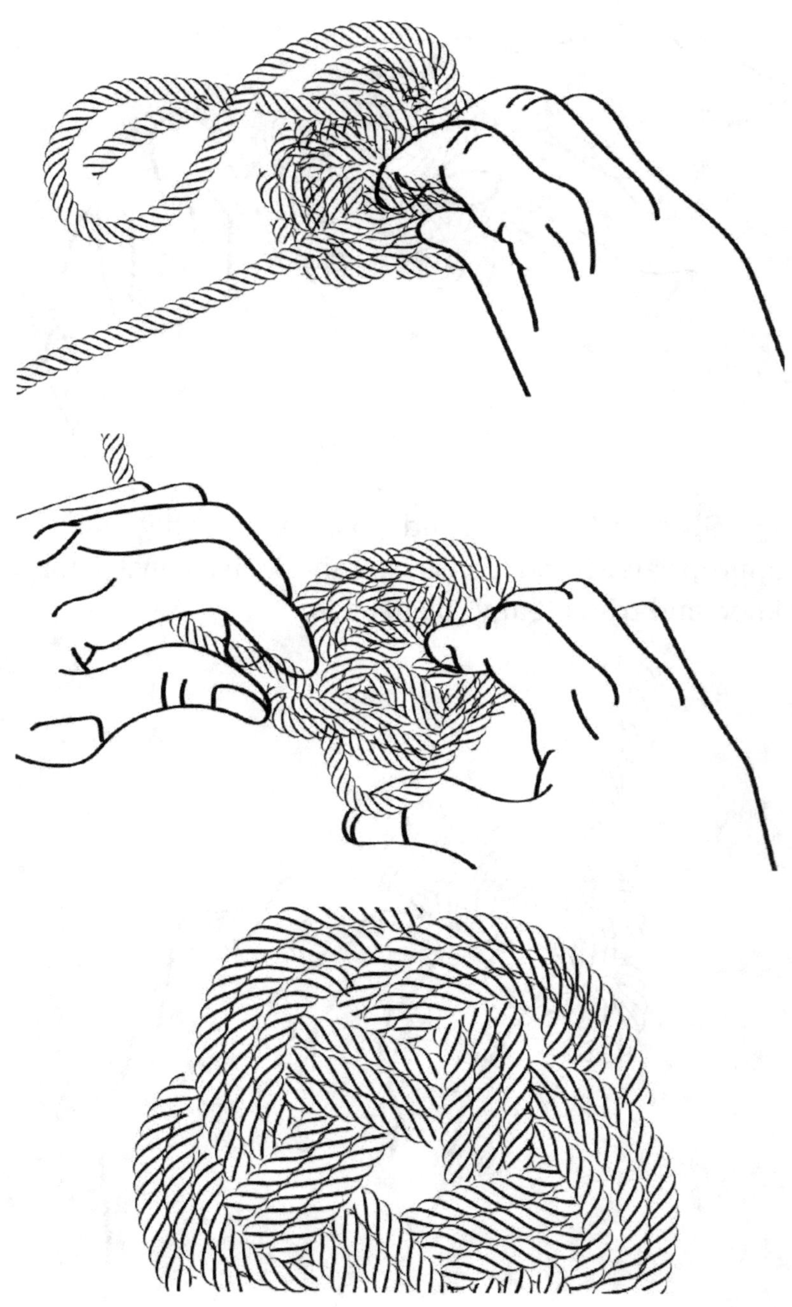

Your Carrick bend mat is complete.

Knots Based on Carrick Bend

The Carrick Mat: The Carrick mat is a decorative woven knot typically used for pads and mats that consists of Carrick connected by their ends to form an endless knot.

Diamond Knot: Starting as a Carrick bend, the diamond knot is tied in a pattern that allows all ends to emerge opposite and parallel to their respective standing point.

Mooring Hitch

The mooring hitch is a simple knot that can be released quickly with just a pull at the tag end. However, it is more secure than the slippery hitch knot, and sailors use it for temporarily mooring boats.

You can tie a mooring hitch around a tree, pole, or anywhere along the length of another rope. Tying a mooring hitch is one of the easiest things to do, and all it takes is just a few steps. These steps are:

Tie a rope to a pole, stick, or tree and pass the string's working end (it can be any of them) through the gap.

- Form a bight with the working end of the rope.

- Pass the bight behind the standing part through the loop created.

- Hold the bight already in the loop and then pull a little to tighten the knot.

- Ensure your release end of the rope is standing out and a bit longer than the other end. Just like that, you have made a Mooring hitch knot.

When you combine the mooring hitch with the butterfly knot, note that it becomes more secure, mostly when used to hold items together.

Friendship Knot

A friendship knot is a beautiful square-shaped and highly secure knot, usually made from other different colors of threads/ropes. It forms part of the eleven essential traditional Chinese knotting craft which originated during the Tang and Song dynasty (960-1279 AD).

Many people use the friendship knot for macramé patterns and tie straps, scarves, ropes, lanyards, ribbons, and paracords. When used on fuzzy or twisted strings, they tend to come out better.

Even in modern times, the friendship knot is very popular, as most scouts and guides are seen wearing their neckerchiefs in a friendship knot style, instead of the usual woggle.

Surprisingly, you may have seen the friendship knot countless without realizing it. Interestingly, the knot symbolizes the World Association of Girl Guides and Girl Scouts (WAGGGS).

You can also find designs of the friendship knots on jewelry, tattoos, and even art pieces. A friendship knot symbolizes the bond and beauty of friendship. It also represents a sign of appreciation.

Getting to tie that scarf, rope, or ribbon of yours in a friendship knot is relatively easy, and here are the easy ways to tie a friendship knot.

- Get two straps of alternating colors (optional). Let's assume these colors are black and white.

- Make sure the size of both ends of the strap is equal. They appear symmetrical that way.

- Cross both straps and pass the black under the white strap.

- Take the white end of the strap and place it end down.

- Place the black strap the same way but facing the right to form the letter' Z.'

- Pass the white through the angular loop formed by the 'Z' of the black strand.

- Hold both ends of the straps and pull to tighten the knot.

- Whip or add some glue to prevent having fraying ends.

- Trim off excesses.

Note: If you're using a rope, it's best to get a stiff one to retain the shape.

Your Friendship knot is complete.

Diamond (Lanyard) Knot

Diamond knot, also known as Bosun's whistle, lanyard, or knife lanyard knot, is an intricate knot used to make a decorative or fixed loop at the middle of a cord, which could be a rope, paracord, lanyard, or even leather.

You can use a diamond knot as your zipper pull to make it more secure. You can also use it to create a macramé pattern. Diamond knot designs can also be found on jewelry designs, key chains, knife tassels, and tattoos. You can create a diamond knot using a single or two ropes (although it's usually better with two strands) and then make them into a single knot.

When you see a finished diamond knot, it may appear challenging to implement, and you'd likely make mistakes at the first trial, but with constant practice, you can be perfect at tying the perfect diamond knot. Making a diamond knot is like making a Carrick bend. With these simple instructions, it becomes easier and faster to tie your diamond knot.

- As a beginner, get 2 ft. of rope.

- Form a ring loop with the rope and encircle the loop with the rope.

- Pass one part of the rope through the loop to create another loop.

- Pass the other end through the newly made loop.

- Take the initial end up.

- Pass it through the first loop.

- Now take the other end through the same loop to create a bigger loop.

- Hold and pull the bigger loop and watch all the loops tighten together.

Just like that, your diamond knot is made.

Scaffold Knot

The scaffold knot is sometimes called the triple overhand noose or gallows knot. It closely resembles the hangman noose because it is also a noose knot. The scaffold knot is made to resemble a noose and form a loop that fits snuggly when tied around any object, rail, or bar.

The scallop knot is almost similar to the poacher's knot (also called two-turn or double scaffold), but the difference is that scallop knots are made with an extra turn around the standing end. You should note that you shouldn't tie the scallop knot or any other noose knot around a person's neck as it could prove to be fatal because the breaking strength of a scallop knot is around seventy-five percent.

Don't let that scare you away, though. You can still make a scallop knot when you go hiking or sailing, especially for lifelines and harnesses. Flathead anglers also use the scallop knot when fishing. You can also use the scallop knot to join two ropes together. Because of how secure the knot is, you can attach the knot to a shackle or carabineer to make it easier when climbing.

Tying a scallop knot is quite complicated, but practice makes perfect. Here are easy steps to create a scallop knot.

- Get your rope. Wrap one end of the rope around the standing bight of the rope.

- Wrap that same end twice around the opposite direction to create a loop. Pass the end over the loop.

- Gently take it out parallel to the standing part. After you have done that, hold the loop and pull the end to tighten the loop.

Your scallop knot is complete. You can add a thimble to ensure your knot lasts longer.

You can always adjust the loop by pulling on the longer end to tighten or loosen the knot. Also, sailors used the thimble to prevent the knot from chafing in boats and yachts, which is why it is recommended that you also use a thimble to protect your knot from wear.

Dropper Loop

The dropper loop, which is also known as a dropper knot, is commonly used by fishermen. Many anglers use the dropper loop for deep-sea or bass fishing because it aids them in creating multiple hook bait rings.

A dropper loop is highly secure and a top fishing knot employed by fishermen because it is often useful to attach rubber worms or tube lures above a jig. Even a moderately strong knot can make a small catch like panfish or tiny saltwater species when fishing.

Here are the ways to tie a dropper loop.

- Get a strand. Create a long loop, hold its top, and wrap it around itself. Wrap the loop five more times.

- Pass the top through the center loop. Pull it and stretch the ends (with your mouth) to make your loop tighter.

- Once it is tightened to your desire, your dropper knot is ready to use.

Another way to create your dropper loop is by keeping your first loop while twisting the other end to a matchstick at an overlapping point. Then slid the bigger loop through the tiny one left by the matchstick to form a dropper.

You should know that the number of times you wrap your loop around the straight line determines how tight and small your dropper will appear. If you created the dropper loop for fishing, you should ensure that you test your knot before setting out to fish.

Make sure your loop is very long if you want to set a hook directly to it and reduce the twisting and fouling rate of your fishing line.

Cat's Paw Knot

Cat's Paw Knot is perhaps one of the easiest to tie. It is used to connect a line or rope to a hook, swivel. People, mostly sailors and those who work in the docks or piers, prefer the Cat's Paw Knot because it doesn't jam and is excellent for lifting heavy loads from an angle.

Why Cat's Paw knot is excellent for lifting things is because of the twisted loops. It is more substantial and secure so that even when one end breaks, the other end holds temporarily till the task is completed.

Fishermen also use the Cat's paw knot for loop to loop connection when fishing. You can use the knot to join a braid to another or a mono leader. The Cat's paw can be directly connected to a Bimini Twist. The knot is mentioned in The Ashley Book of Knots.

Here's how to tie a Cat's Paw Knot.

- Create two loops with a bight of rope. Twist each end of the loops around themselves. Repeat the process three times.

- Bring both loops close to each other. Pass a hook across the center of both loops and pull it to tighten the knot.

Just like that, your Cat's Paw Knot is complete.

You don't necessarily have to make use of a rope bight. You can also make a paracord double line or a closed strop to create the knot. Another thing to note is that certain knot modifications tend to have additional twists on both ends of the rope bight.

Poacher's Knot

Also known as the Strangle snare and double overhand noose, the poacher's knot is a highly secure knot that is mainly used to bind items together. One notable thing about this particular knot is that it can be tied even in very slippery ropes made out of Spectra and Dyneema because other types of loop knots will quickly come undone when tied on these ropes.

Poachers commonly used it for hunting for birds and other small animals. You use the knot to connect a rope to a carabiner as a hitch or part of a snag. Cat paw's knot can also be used to form a simple snare. Along with the scaffold knot, the poacher's knot can be made stronger and is ideal for tying a foot loop to a hand ascender.

Here's how to Tie a Poacher's Knot.

- Wrap the tag end around a rope bight. Repeat the process once, take it up, and pass it through the two loops.

- Pull both ends of the loop to tighten the knot.

Do not make the mistake of making just one turn around the standing part. When you do that, you're only making an ordinary overhand knot, which isn't strong enough to lift heavy objects. If there is enough tag, you can add a stopper knot for more strength and security.

Hangman's Knot (Noose)

The hangman knot or noose, as the name indicates, was used originally for the execution of prisoners. It is believed to have been invented in the United Kingdom. Recently, its uses have diversified for fishing and boating. Anglers use the knot to attach a swivel, lure, or hook to their fishing line. Sailors and hikers also use the knot to tie down a boat, tent, or vehicle because of its self-tightening quality.

People like to make it for Halloween decorations and other artistic purposes. The knot is also employed when making bracelets and paracord knife lanyards. The loop formed by the strong knot is adjustable.

Remember, never use this knot on any human, whether in a playful manner or not, because the loop could tighten accidentally even when tied loosely and can prove fatal.

Knowing that, let's get into the process of creating a Hangman's knot. Here is how you can tie a Hangman's knot/noose.

- Make an '8' shape with your rope and pass the tag end behind the '8' form you made.

- Then wrap the end around the upper loop and the standing part of the rope. Repeat the process three times.

- Pass the stationary part through the small top loop. Hold the lower loop and pull the tag end to tighten the loop.

After that, your Hangman's knot is complete.

Butterfly Knot

Also referred to as the Alpine Butterfly knot or Lineman's Loop, the Butterfly knot is used mainly for rock climbing and glacier travel because it holds the climber in the middle when two or more people move up a rope.

It is also used to attach a carabiner to the climbing harnesses. There is also the Double Butterfly Knot, which is quite similar to the regular butterfly knot, but the difference is that the knot has two side by side loops instead of one.

Double butterfly knot offers the same highly secure knot since it has the advantage of providing two slip points instead of one. The Butterfly knot is regarded as one of the most secure knots, and it is also one of the easiest to tie.

Following just three simple steps, you have completed the Butterfly knot, and these steps are:

- Form an '8' shaped loop and fold the upper loop down. Pull it around and pass the upper loop through the lower loop.

- Pull both loops to tighten the knot.

You just made a butterfly knot.

Valdotain Tresse

People used this knot initially in Alpine rescue, from where it graduated into being a famous arborist knot. Climbers use the VT knot to ascend and descend ropes when climbing. Valdotain Tresse is used to attach a carabiner to a climbing rope. It is also best for rock climbing and caving. You can use the VT knot for canyoneering and when engaging in technical rescue activity. The knot is also great as a rappel device, and you can use the knot for slacklining.

One unique thing about the VT knot is that you can always release the knot under load. Tying a Valdotain Tresse knot isn't a small feat for a beginner because it could cause death or other severe damage to people and property if not appropriately secured. Hence extra care needs to be taken when making a Valdotain Tresse. You must follow guidelines for tying the knot to ensure that there is no mistake.

The VT knot can be with a rope with two sewn or spliced eyes (or split tail friction cord) or hand-tied loops. Here are the steps on how to tie a Valdotain Tresse.

- Wrap both tag ends around your rope bight.

- Pass it through the two loops created. Pull both ends to tighten.

- Wrap the right end loop four times around the blue rope. Pass the blue rope down from the backside.

- Wrap it once around the red rope again. Wrap the left end of the red rope around the blue rope.

- Pass both ends through a carabiner.

- Close the carabineer to complete the knot.

Once you make your VT knot, test its effectiveness using different diameters, lengths, and friction cord materials. One interesting fact about the VT knot is that step one to three are also the same way you can make a Poacher's knot.

Chapter Summary

- Celtic pattern coasters are the best way to put those bits and pieces to good use.

- They are handy, beautiful, and fun to design.

Intermediate Guide to Celtic Patterns

Introduction

This book—Intermediate Guide to Celtic Patterns—will sharpen your skills, teach you how to use the basic knowledge you already acquired, push you further along the journey, and turn you into a pro in no time. Prepare your mind for several Celtic projects you never knew existed. Since these projects come with easy step-by-step analysis, you can also create your own designs and "up your skills" a bit.

Are you ready? In this book, you will learn how to incorporate your Celtic patterns into calligraphy, how to integrate these patterns to clothing, how to master your Celtic knots, secret grid techniques you can use to sketch your Celtic patterns, how you can design your own Celtic patterns, and how to sketch Celtic maze patterns. Also, by the time you finish this book, you will understand the fundamentals of illuminated manuscripts, and how to create one, as well as how to integrate zoomorphic knotwork animals into your Celtic artwork, how to create a double Celtic knot paracord, a Celtic monkey fist, and a Celtic knot keychain. Other things you'll learn include how to create colorful mandala projects, and how to use pencil colors to draw khala patterns.

Intermediate Guide to Celtic Patterns, like a traveler's compass, offers clear direction on how you can become a pro in Celtic designs in a short time. Your journey to stardom starts here.

Chapter One:
Celtic Calligraphy

Call it "Celtic Calligraphy" or "Celtic Knots" and you are on point. These knots are actually embellishments often used to create unique designs on clothes and other home decorations. Remnants of these knots are everywhere many years after Celtic civilization hit a standstill. Still, more societies are embracing the Celtic culture, and its influence on the modern world is growing out of control. Celtic knots mean many things to many people but this depends on the overriding culture of the place where the knots are used. Some of these knots symbolize loyalty, love, friendship, and faith. With just a thread, people have used Celtic knots to symbolize how life and eternity are intertwined. Celtic knots, being complex decorative designs, have been extensively used to beautify items such as cutlery, clothing, mugs, plates, and jewelry sets.

A look back at ancient history will help us understand what Celtic knots really stand for. Back around 450 A.D., Christians began to influence Celtic civilization by creating Christian manuscripts and artwork that incorporated plants, animals, and humans. Knot patterns were being used to decorate artefacts, illuminated pages, clothes, and other finished items, not just during the mediaeval times for the Gaelic Celts. Often, these patterns went with beautiful and amazing calligraphy. Still, religious people, apart from Christian and Muslim faithfuls, also had Celtic designs that met their needs.

Celtic knot designs can enhance seamless and elaborate fabrics and other finished items. Their well laid out grids, lines, symmetrical patterns, and flowing letterforms could be all you need to make your finished items spectacular. Are you wondering about how to create knot designs as infill for decorative initials? No worries. Celtic knot designs, like other artworks, are shaped by your innate ability and talent, not just basic or historical principles or skills. Fine, you could learn the principles or practice the original skills, but your creative ingenuity determines how far you will go. Power the principles with personal creativity and you will create great knot designs.

Think about the complexity of the Celtic knots you want to create. See what you need to put in place to achieve it. Sure, it is not something you can achieve in a hurry. You need to exercise some patience as you try to work things out. Some knots, if not all, require certain mathematical structures and principles. So, you need to understand how these structures work before you can create an amazing Celtic knot. Take your time to create elaborate and complex knot patterns you want. Are you wondering about the number of hours it would take you to create a Celtic knot? Designing a Celtic knot could take you 30 minutes, one hour, one day, or many weeks, depending on the size of the design, the number of tiny lines you draw per minute, and how long it takes you to color the tiny boxes you have created.

Gradually, as you draw your Celtic designs, you will really enjoy the process because it is a relaxing and meditative activity. Your level of alertness and creativity will determine how well you handle and enjoy the repetitive movements of creating your favorite knots. Scanners and image software can be used to manipulate and reproduce several sections of Celtic knots rapidly, especially when you are in a hurry to create choice Celtic designs. Some people enjoy the action of drawing by hand, while others love to have the help technology can offer. However, if you really want to master Celtic knots, you need to practice drawing them and really understanding how they are composed structurally.

Popular Celtic Knots and What They Stand For

Celtic knots look good. There is no doubt about that. People have been enjoying these knots as early as the 3rd century. Each knot has its peculiar significance and trying to understand or interpret these knots, without adequate records about their unique symbols, could pose a huge challenge. Today, what we know about Celtic knots is determined by how much access to facts we have had. For example, you might have seen a Celtic Knot on stones in burial sites, and conclude that such knots represent faith or unity among certain people. Also, you might have heard people say that some knots could ward off evil spirits. Yes, they could be right because Celtic patterns in tombs usually reference eternal life or eternity. A Celtic knot has a line that runs continuously without an end. Here, I will show you a few well known Celtic Knots and what they symbolize.

1. Celtic Cross: Being a spiritual symbol, the Celtic cross was used in ancient times to reference the Sun God. Soon, Christians began to see the circle around the cross as God's eternal love for men. Several Celtic crosses of the 3rd and 4th centuries still exist in our modern-day world, and these unique crosses now cut across cultures and religions.

2. Trinity Knot: Triquetra, also known as the trinity knot, was used to honor the neo-pagan triple goddess. But lately, Christians have used it for their 'The Father, The Son, and The Holy Spirit' doctrine. Again, Irish jewelry designers and silversmiths have embellished their products with the trinity knot to showcase the everlasting love of the Irish people.

3. Tree of Life: Already the Irish symbol of nature, the tree of life is one of the most popular Celtic knots around the world. Its flowing form represents the balanced and harmonious natural world.

4. Celtic Love Knot: Feel free to call it the Anam Cara knot or the Celtic love knot. Its two intertwined hearts symbolize friendship and

wisdom. It is an infinite pattern and it represents everlasting love.

5. Sailor's Knot: This knot comes with endless loops made up of two woven ropes. Sailors would weave ropes to remember their loved ones just before they started their journey on the open seas. Again, these knots signified a love that would never break.

6. Shield Knot: Celts believed that shield knots could protect them from evil spirits, both at home and on the battlefield. Shield knots could come in circular or square shapes and they have two spiral knots, apart from the spiral and triple spiral knots.

7. Spiral Knot: Spiral knots have varied meanings depending on where you find their engravings, and they could symbolize a journey from the physical world to the after-life, also known as the spiritual life. For example, spiral knots found at grave sites or passage tombs would represent a spiritual passage to the world beyond.

8. Triple Spiral: Triple spiral knots are trinity designs and they usually represent land, sea, and sky, our natural world.

How to Incorporate Celtic Pattern into Calligraphy

There are a few ways to create Celtic patterns, but all the methods are subject to grid layouts and diagonal line placement. So, how do you incorporate your Celtic pattern knowledge into calligraphy? It's easy. Here's how to do it.

Required Materials

- Paper

- 2.5 mm wide fountain pen

- Steady hands

Instructions

Follow these simple steps to incorporate your celtic pattern into calligraphy.

1. Consider the alphabets and try to memorize what they look like. The alphabets share a few features such as a line in the middle and 2 commas on either side, different sides, or on the alphabets. So, before you do anything, take your time to study the alphabet because it can aid the process.

2. Set a nib angle of your pen while you run the calligraphy.

3. Station the angle of your pen while running the
    calligraphy.

4. Move your pen all at once. Don't lean on it.

Just follow these instructions to do effortless
Celtic calligraphy. Be creative. The level of your
creativity will determine the beauty of your Celtic
patterns. Again, you need to exercise a great deal of
patience. It is hard to be creative without patience. So,
develop great Celtic knot ideas, and dedicate your
time to actualizing your beautiful ideas.

Chapter Summary

- Celtic knots are embellishments used in
  creating unique designs and clothes.

- Creativity is the sole determinant of how
  beautiful a Celtic design can be.

- All Celtic knots have natural and spiritual
  meanings. For example, the trinity knot was a
  neo-pagan triple goddess but was later used by
  Christians to represent 'The Father, The Son,
  and The Holy Spirit.'

In the next chapter you will learn how to use
Celtic patterns to embellish your quilts and clothes.↓

Chapter Two:
Celtic Patterns for Needlework Embellishment, Clothing and Quilts

Celtic patterns are very attractive on every fabric. No wonder people around the world continue to use these patterns to decorate and embellish their trousers, skirts, tops, and jewelry. Use these patterns to embellish your fabrics, and feel free to paint, draw, or even sew them onto your fabrics, and you'll surely love the outcome. In this chapter, you'll learn how to incorporate Celtic patterns on your clothing. Always try to learn the basics of anything you want to do— be it needle felting, serging, or needlework embellishments. Draw on your experience with other crafts to bring your skills to the table. You might want to explore free-motion quilting because it is one of the easiest ways to get started.

How to Draw a Celtic Knot Pattern

Celtic knots are beautiful ornate decorative knots. These super attractive knots are without beginning or end but often take elaborate twists and turns, making some people assume that it is difficult to create. I will show you how to draw these knots for your needlework embellishment, clothing, quilts, and other projects. So, ready a pencil, graph paper, a ruler, and a colored pencil as we get into drawing a few Celtic patterns. Ready your mind and focus on the steps I will be sharing with you shortly because Celtic patterns are complicated. You need 100% concentration and consistent practice to be an expert designer of Celtic knots. With the step-by-step analysis provided here and a few screenshots added, you won't have issues perfecting your Celtic patterns.

1. Draw a rectangle of dots at the corners of your graph paper, as shown below. Here, I created 9 by 7 rectangular dots.

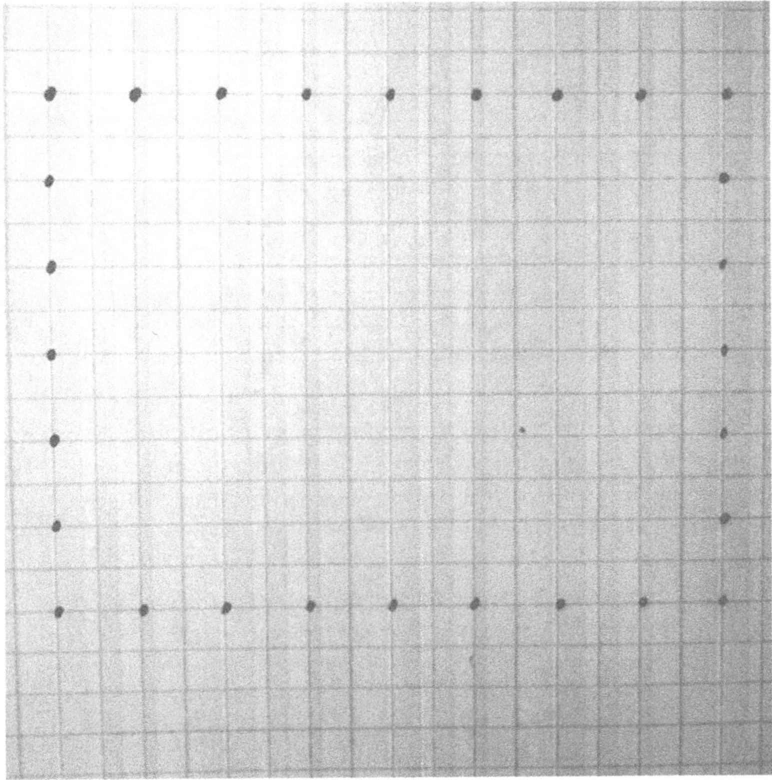

2. Create another set of dots directly under the
    first dots with your colored pencil.

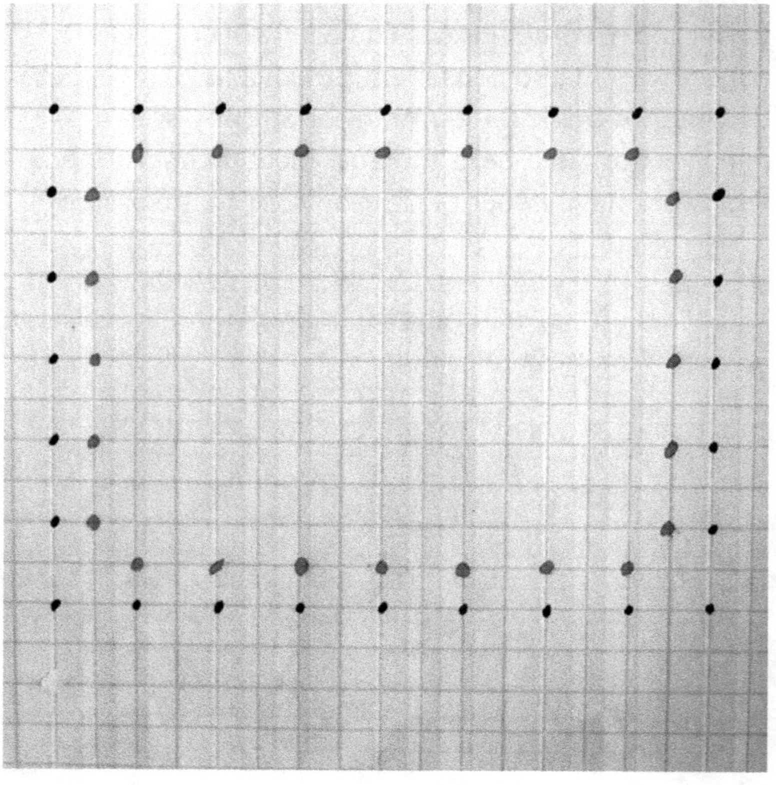

3. Connect the colored dots with your ruler to create diagonal lines.

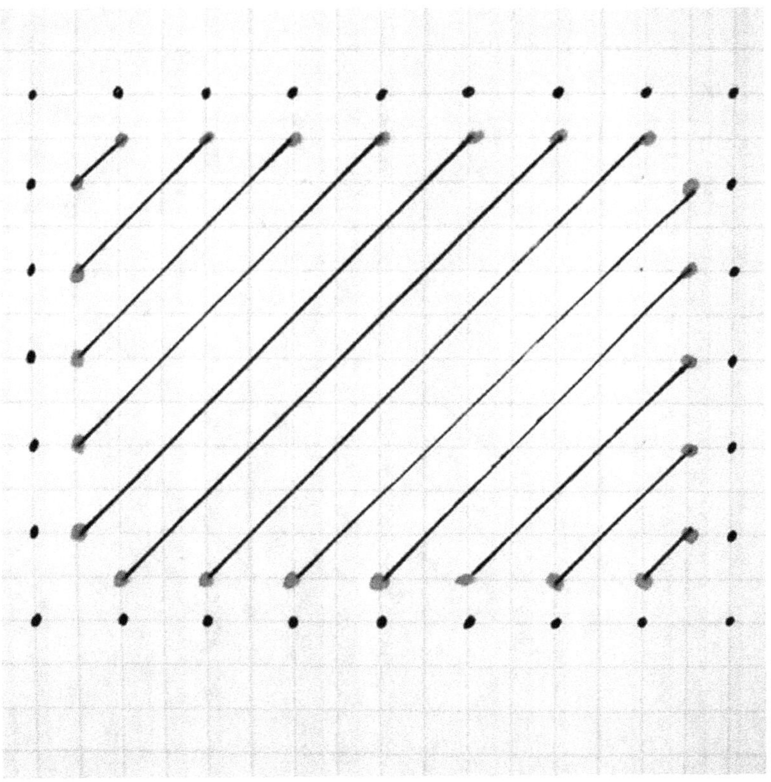

4. Connect the colored dots on the opposite side to create a grid filling

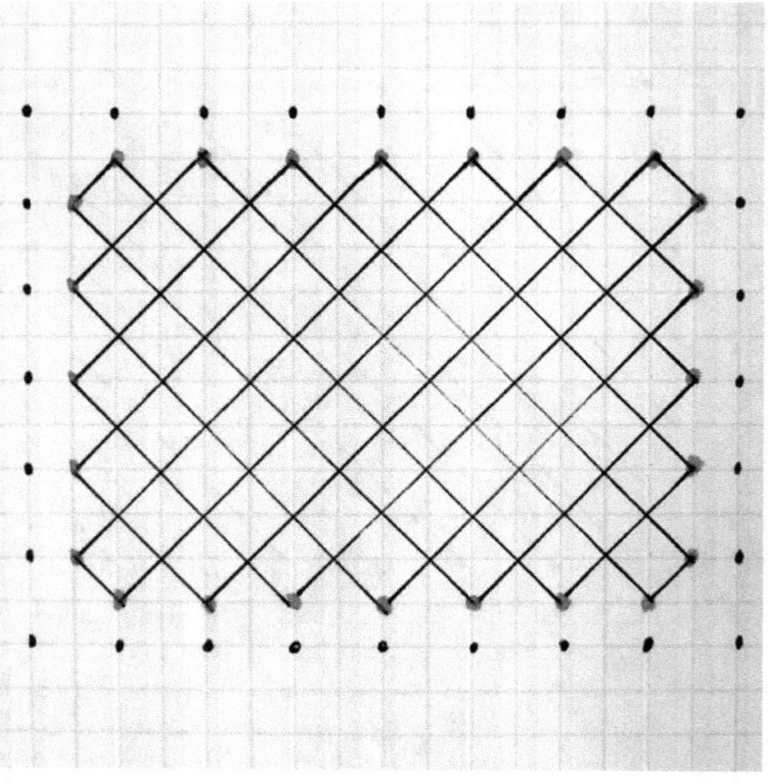

5. Draw the outer edge.

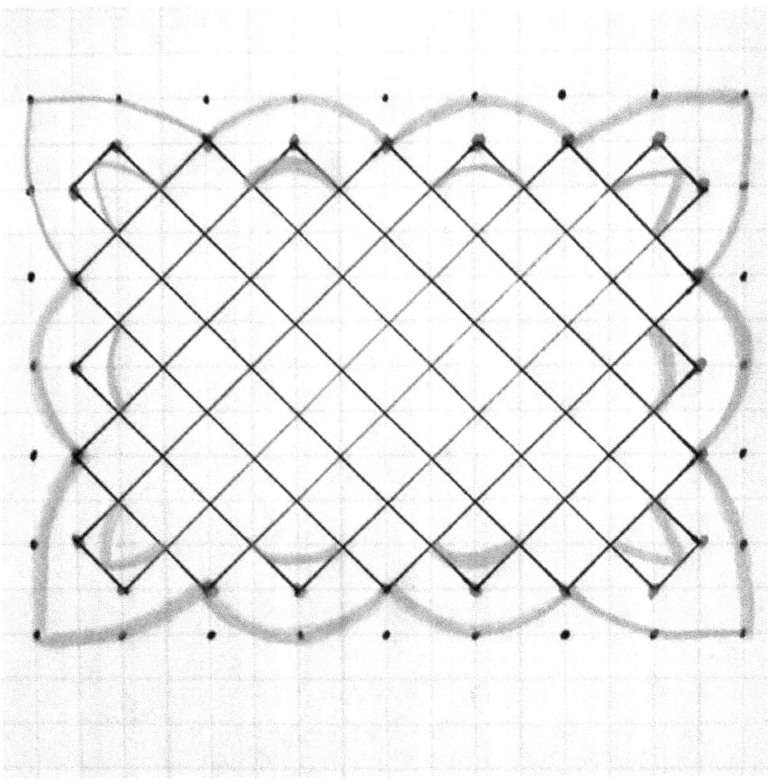

I used a different colored pencil to draw these new lines so that you could see them clearly. So, try to draw the lines with your own pencil. Start from the 4 corners and link the line from your second colored dot to the second pencil dot and the outside corner dot. Allow this line to connect the second pencil dot and the second colored dot. Next, draw inner curves or corners under all the newly created lines. Confused? It's hard to explain this step with words but no worries. Just pay keen attention to the image.

6. Clean up the unused hard corners or curves.

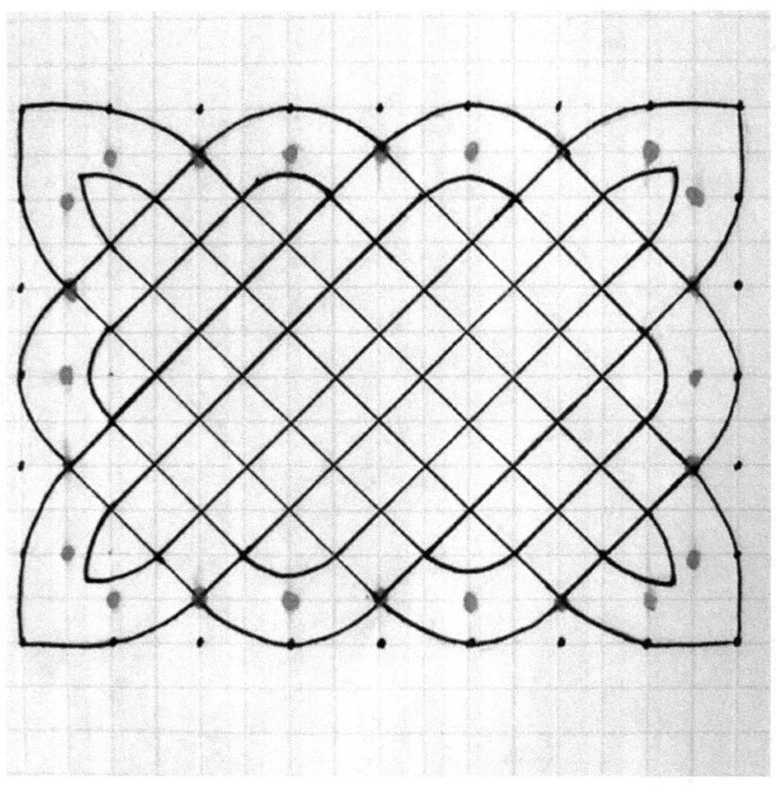

7. Begin to weave the lines.

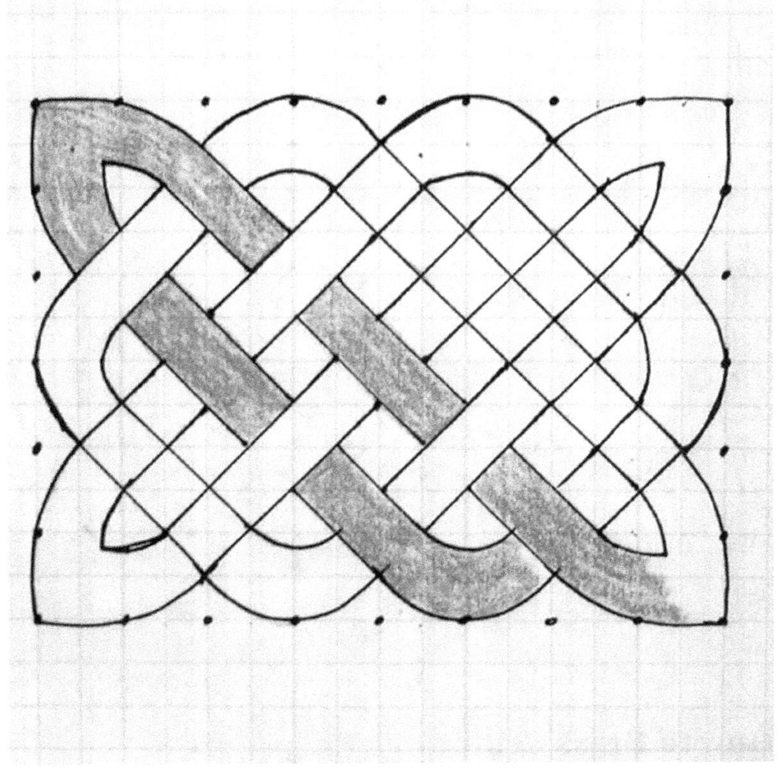

Here, I decided to add color so that you could easily see exactly what I was doing. You only need to erase some lines. Pay attention to how I erased a few lines to create some enticing weaving effects. Continue weaving until you clean up all the lines and get back to where you actually started from.

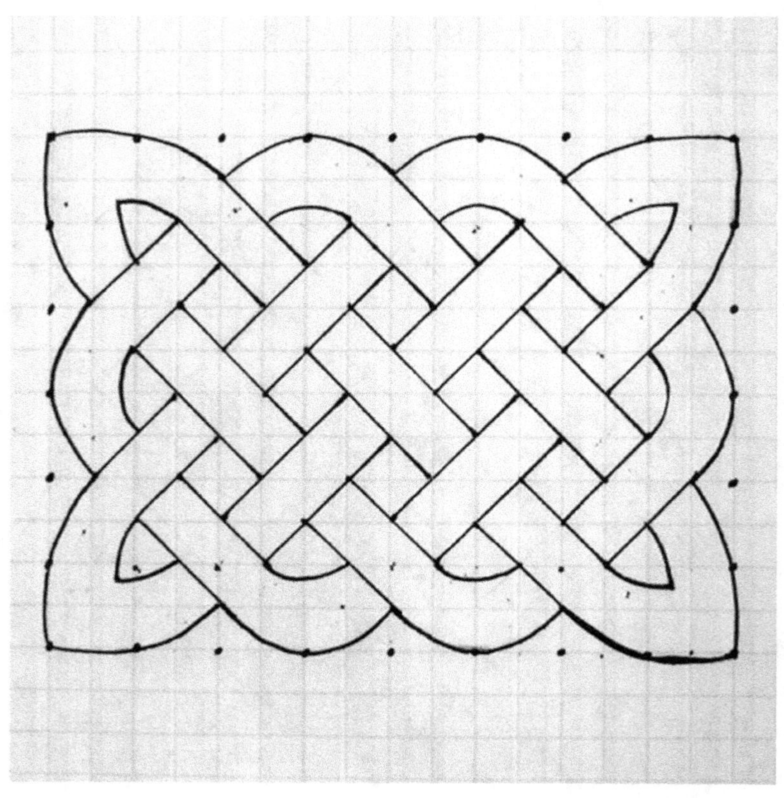

How to Dress Celtic

Celtic knot patterns are so unique and beautiful that most people go for clothes and jewelry adorned with these lovely knots. No wonder the number of people asking for Celtic designs around the world is always on the increase. Some people adopt Celtic attire because of their love for unique and beautiful clothes or just to connect with their ancestors. One thing you just can't ignore about the Celtic lifestyle is the beauty of their knot patterns. Here are a few things to note before you can adopt the perfect Celtic dressing lifestyle.

1. Research clothing styles: Take your time to see a few images of Celtic artistic depictions to know the ones that work for you. It is not just seeing the images. You need to study them and opt for the styles that suit you. Remember that choice of clothing styles is relative. Don't order because you saw some positive comments about the style. Make purchases when you are sure that the style is perfect for you. You can get these images through Google Images or Pinterest. Also, these search engines have great Celtic ideas for modern clothing.

2. Study the dressing style of Celtic nations: Consider knowing a few things about the dressing style of Ireland, Scotland, Wales, Cornwall, Brittany, and Isle of Man, being the six known Celtic nations. Feel free to add their thrilling attires to your wardrobe. While kilts are great for daring men, the Scottish tartan fits most everyday clothing.

3. Opt for choice Celtic ornaments: Celtic jewelry is readily available for purchase online. The iconic Celtic cross would be great if you are a Christian or you want something that emphasizes the Christian faith. Non-Christians or anyone who doesn't like a cross could simply go for the trisilicon or the torque. Again, you can check Wikipedia or other search engines to see available Celtic ornaments.

4. Purchase original Celtic clothing: Don't be in a hurry to purchase your Celtic clothes. Make sure you are looking for quality and affordability. Sites such as Amazon and Etsy house all sorts of Celtic shirts, sweaters, scarves, tee-shirts, and hats. Also, this clothing come with the names and designs of the Celtic nations already listed to pick from.

5. Choose the right shapes and colors: Consider your favorite color and shape before you place orders for Celtic clothes. Most men opt for black and green tartan trousers. But, if such colors do not thrill you, go for what you are comfortable with. The Iron Age Celtic tradition does not allow women to wear trousers. Instead, there are several long and short skirts you can wear as a woman. Again, depending on your favorite color, most women go for green or brown Celtic skirts. Modest dressing with a traditional look is fundamental to the Celtic culture. Also, buttoned-up green, black, or brown vests on collared shirts could spice up your outfit.

6. Opt for the right shoes: It depends on the outlook you want to achieve. Medieval-looking shoes or boots will make you look authentic while green chuck taylors would keep you happy all day. Also, green, black, red, or brown ballet-flat or river-dancing shoes are perfect for most women.

Other Celtic designs for body decoration include shamrocks, dragons, Ogham writing, Celtic cross, and ravens. Feel free to draw or tatoo these designs on your skin.

Traditional Celtic knots and patterns found in art books can be used for modern embellishments. How? Just use the techniques in those art books to embellish your cuffs, collars, pockets, and other finished items. Map out your work before you create the designs or you'll have difficulty creating the required embellishments. No worries. Just follow these guidelines and the whole thing will be very easy for you.

Plan Your Motif

It is easier to start with patch pockets because you can tilt their rectangular shape to fit the design you want to create. So, to get started, you need to collect a hand-sewing needle, sewing thread, a few pins, basting thread, a permanent marking pen, pattern paper, and enough charmeuse to create bias tubes. Next, follow this procedure:

1. Draw or choose your favorite pattern: It is fine if you can get an existing pattern, but, if you don't have one to work with, you'll have to draw your own pattern. Drawing your own pattern will take time but you'll get it right after a few trials. Still, finding knot patterns should be easy because they are readily available

online. Simply use Google Image, Pinterest or other search engines to locate them.

2. Make several copies of your favorite pattern: Don't settle for only a copy of the pattern. No! Remember you will have to adjust the pattern a few times to get the actual shape you want. Should you need to expand the width of a Celtic pattern, just overlap the original pattern with the one already shaped to size. Again, make sure that you align the base and the added pattern.

3. Practice with bias tubes: Take your time to experiment with the tubes to see how the design turns out. Again, don't just focus a single pattern. Try to practice a few patterns to see how fast you are learning the process. Also, pay keen attention to stitching gauge and knitting.

Make The Tubes

Cut out enough seam allowances for the bias tubes or you'll experience sewing difficulties. Since most patch pockets' tubes are 1/4 inch wide, this tip will aid the process of making the tubes.

1. Cut the charmeuse bias 1 1/2 inches wide: Consider your favorite design and the size of the pockets you want to make before you opt for any silk charmeuse fabric. Cut your bias to size once.

2. Remove the stretch: Iron each end of the strips to remove the stretch. However, you need to pull the strip a little bit as you iron to avoid creating other stretch patterns.

3. Sew the tubes: Align the long sides and fold the stripes on the right sides. Stitch 1/4 inch away from the fold but make sure you stretch the fabric a little bit while you are sewing the tubes. Once you're done with this row, stitch another row one inch away from the first one. Afterwards, you feel free to trim the fabric around the stitching line until your desired shape and size is attained.

4. Press the tube flat: Use a tube turner to flatten the right side of the tubes. Again, feel free to use your favorite flattening method if the tube turner does not work for you.

Get a Template Where You Can Stitch the Design

It is time to turn your paper design into a template you could use to map your tubes. Here is what you need to do.

1. Transfer the motif: Place the design on a pattern paper and use a permanent marking pen to trace it. Ensure that the whole design is clear on the paper so that you can see the various crossovers and intersections of the design.

2. Place a tube over the template: Focus more on the panel, not the edges, or you'll end up joining the tubes and the whole thing will be messed up. Pin the template on the tube from the start of an intersection to its end.

3. Baste the tube: Be careful not to stitch the intersection lines of tubes while you baste the tube. Run this process continuously until you baste the whole design.

4. Stitch the intersections: Tack the basted tubes at their intersection points. Ensure that none of the stitches is showing at the other side of the fabric.

5. Finish the panel: Get the basting threads off the template and steam the design for some minutes, and hand-stitch the design to your pocket.

Chapter Summary

- Celtic patterns can be used to decorate trousers, skirts, tops, and jewelry.

- You can download your favorite Celtic patterns online or simply design one from scratch.

The next chapter is all about you mastering your Celtic knots. See you there.↓

Chapter Three: Master Your Celtic Knots

Celtic knots are beautiful designs that anyone can create in the comfort of their homes. They can be scary if it's your first attempt to draw them. Gradually, as you continue to create these decorative artworks, you will begin to master them and everything will become very easy for you. These knots can enhance your work with little or no effort at all. You really don't have to be an expert at drawing before you can create amazing Celtic knots. No! Just a few guidelines and you'll be good to go. However, to master these Celtic knots, you need to embrace constant practice. Soon, you will learn how to draw some Celtic knots, but before then, pay keen attention to these instructions if you really want to master how to create different Celtic knots.

1. Learn to draw straight lines: Celtic knots involve so many straight lines and there's no way you can master these knots if you still have issues drawing straight lines. So, begin to practice drawing straight lines.

2. Practice drawing different categories of curves: Celtic knots involve several horizontal and vertical curves. You just have to understand how to draw these curves before you can create

your favorite knots. How will you master these curves without constant practice?

3. Learn to vary the width and height of a curve: Celtic knots come in different sizes and shapes, you'll need to either increase or decrease the width and height of your curves. So, the earlier you start learning how to do this, the better it is for you.

4. Begin to visualize in 3D: You need to create a 3D map of the Celtic knots you want to draw. So, if you don't know how to do it, learn it. You can search YouTube for videos on how to create 3D maps of Celtic knots.

5. Visualize overlap, top, and bottom lines: Early planning is good for every task, including Celtic knots. Take your time to visualize how the whole thing will turn out before you start drawing, especially if it is the first time you're creating a Celtic knot. Make sure you decide the lines to overlap and those that will occupy the top and bottom position.

6. Practice shading: Sure, you will have to shade your pattern to reflect your favorite look. Decide in advance the color you want to use. Again, if you're confused on how to properly shade your pattern, feel free to check online videos and tutorials on Celtic knots' shading.

7. Learn to add shadows: While shading the Celtic knot, you might want to create a shadow effect in a particular area of the knot. There are several online aids for people who do not know how to add shadows to their Celtic knots. Find these aids and learn how to do it properly.

Pay keen attention to the above tips if you want to draw faultless Celtic knots.

How to Draw the Celtic Tree of Life Knot

The Celtic tree of life looks complex but you'll have no problem drawing it if you can break it into steps. First, draw the large curly branches before you begin to add the smaller ones. Once everything is set, add the fun, finishing decorative shapes. Here is all you need to create a perfect Celtic tree of life.

Required Materials

- Drawing paper

- Black marker

- Crayons

Instructions

Follow these steps to draw your Celtic tree of life in just an hour:

1. Draw the two curly sides of a tree and add the top curvy branches.

2. Sketch the lower branches and the ground lines before you add the two center branches.

3. Add smaller branches from the bottom of the tree until you get to the top.

4. Add your favorite decorative shapes such as spots, mushrooms, rectangles, and triangles, as well as flowers and other decorations to the ground of the tree.

5. Use the marker to trace the tree before you add color using your crayons.

How to Draw a Celtic Love Knot

Celtic love knot is also known as the heart knot and it represents affections and everlasting love. Follow these steps to draw your own Celtic heart knot in the comfort of your home.

1. Sketch a heart. Right at the top of the heart you'll see the point joining the two sides. Draw two lines down, one for each side, form the point to create a diamond.

2. Create three slightly curved interlocking lines from the diamond.

3. Sketch another heart beside the first heart. Locate the point that joins the two sides at the top and connect the line on the left with the first heart, while the line on the left rests on the right line.

4. Use the slightly curved lines created in Step 2 to form three arrow points. Allow only the line on the right of the other heart to overlap the arrow points.

Make sure there are no line breaks. Keep all your lines straight.

How to Draw Celtic Trinity Knot

Celtic trinity knots are common designs for Christian faithfuls and non-Christians, and you can draw these knots at your comfort by following these simple steps.

1. Draw a dividing line. Place one dot each at top, lower left, and lower right parts of the dividing line.

2. Sketch a big arc at the top dot and let it ache slightly to the left dot and the right of the dividing line.

3. From the top dot, draw another arc and let it ache slightly down towards the left of the dividing line, before it crosses to the right dot.

4. Connect the left and right dots to the big arc to create the trinity knot.

5. Draw another trinity knot on the inside of the dividing line but make sure the width is equal all through.

6. Erase intersecting lines and add your favorite color to spice it up.

How to Draw the Celtic Cross Knot

Celtic cross knot, just like the trinity knot, is a common design for Christians, and it is easy to draw. Feel free to draw your favorite Celtic cross in the comfort of your home by following these steps.

1. Draw a circle that can surround the cross. Take your time to examine the size of the cross before you sketch this circle.

2. Sketch a smaller circle on a parallel line with the first circle.

3. Draw a small circle in the middle of the previous circles.

4. Sketch the arms of the Celtic cross design. Draw divergent horizontal curved lines by the side of the circle in the middle of the previous circles. Join the horizontal lines on each end to form scalloped patterns, before you sketch an L-shaped line on each of the arms. Again, draw a pair of curved and vertically diverged lines to join the scalloped patterns.

5. Sketch another L-shaped line for each horizontal arm, with the line at the base of the arm. Also, draw two divergent curved lines down from the horizontal arms but make sure

that the two lines are longer than the arms. Join all the lines with a scalloped line at the base.

6. Sketch the knot pattern on each horizontal arm, and create two rounded yet opposite teardrop shapes with a few curved lines. Draw a smaller teardrop shape to overlap the opposite ones.

7. Sketch your knot pattern in the horizontal arms. Draw an overlapping teardrop for each knot. Also, sketch the knot pattern at the bottom of the Celtic cross.

8. Erase all overlapping lines and apply your favorite color on the Celtic cross.

What inspires you to create the Celtic knot? Sure, you don't just jump out your bed in the morning to design some Celtic knots without being motivated to do so. Alexander Babich, MacoshDesign manager, confessed that he was inspired to design Celtic knots after he watched an animated film, 'The Secret of Kells.' The main character in the film did some crazy Celtic patterns and designs and Babich was inspired to create his own Celtic designs. He later said that creating Celtic knots is just like solving a puzzle. It can turn out to be complicated, incredible, and amazing. So, just like Babich, you too need to identify the source of your inspiration. Why? Inspiration is what fuels your passion to design your favorite Celtic knots, as well as what keeps you going. So, after you have

identified what inspires you, what is the next step?
Draw your favorite Celtic knot.

Chapter Summary

- Celtic decorative artworks can be designed in the comfort of your home by using determination and creativity.

- Locate what inspires you to create Celtic patterns to make them attractive and appealing.

You just learned how to master Celtic knots. The next chapter captures secret grid techniques for drawing Celtic patterns.↓

Chapter Four:
Secret Grid Technique to Draw Patterns

Apparently, being an intermediate designer, you have already drawn more than a dozen Celtic patterns over the years. But you often ask yourself why some of these patterns were slightly different from what you really wanted to draw. You are not alone. Hundreds of designers face this challenge daily. Still, use the grid method to achieve accuracy in your drawings. Here is all you need to do to apply the grid technique to draw accurate and efficient Celtic patterns.

Required Materials

- A gridded paper

- A black pen

- Pencil

- An eraser

How to Draw the Pattern

1. Draw the grids: The number of grids to draw depends on the Celtic pattern you want to work on. Take your time to carefully consider the shape and size of the pattern. Ensure that the height and length of the pattern carry an equal

number of grids. Still, you may only need to draw 3 overlay grids—primary, secondary, and tertiary grids.

a. Just draw a few dots to create the primary grid but make sure the dots are vertically and horizontally aligned. Besides that, you need to make sure that the dots are evenly spaced. Better still, use a primary grid of 15 dots wide and 5 dots high. Place a dot in the middle of the primary units to create the secondary grid. Find a way to differentiate primary and secondary grids when you are working with a single color.

b. The tertiary grid shows the path of the pattern. It connects the primary and secondary grids to form a diagonal line. Draw the diagonal lines slightly because you will soon erase them. Again, maintain equal space between the diagonal lines and the other two grids.

2. Draw the breaks: Breaks are lines that show the path of the pattern. Practically, these lines appear on the primary or secondary grids but they should be lightly drawn. Follow these rules to draw the breaks appropriately.

c. Just as the outside edges of your primary grid define the boundary of the pattern, they also serve as breaks.

d. Breaks can be vertical or horizontal, not diagonal.

e. Breaks on primary and secondary grids do not always intersect but two primary or two secondary breaks may intersect.

f. Use a pen or pencil to draw the breaks. Feel free to use a single color for the breaks, but make sure that primary and secondary grids do not intersect.

3. Draw the path: Remember that the breaks act as the path. Again, primary and secondary grids must not intersect. Pay keen attention to these tips before you attempt to draw the path.

g. Straighten the path to the tertiary grid but don't hit the break.

h. Trace the path back to the tertiary grid once you have avoided the break.

i. Some break patterns could have rare or strange pathways but don't allow that to mislead you. Use the tips above and you'll have no difficulty creating the path for your primary and secondary grids.

4. Smoothen the path: You will make two turns when you draw the path— 45 and 90 degree turns. The 45 degree turn is a wide one while the 90 degree turn is a little bit light. So, just

try to sharpen the right turns and round over
the wide Ines. Again, learn how to follow the
path efficiently to create the Celtic pattern
efficiently. Still, you can make the path round
or smooth automatically while you are drawing
the pattern. Feel free to shape the path round
or sharp as you want.

5. Erase overlapping lines: It is easy to mess
    things up at this point especially if you are in
    haste to erase overlapping lines. Take your
    time to carefully check where the path crosses a
    line or when there is a pencil line to erase.

You have just created your pattern.

Why the Grid Drawing Technique?

Grid drawing technique helps you focus on a
particular section of an image or pattern at a time. It
makes efficient drawing easy, although some
designers struggle to use it because they think grid
technique is cheating. No! Grid is just one of the
practical drawing techniques anyone can use to create
complex designs efficiently, and quickly too. Again,
designers, like people in other fields, are not
magicians. They could opt for drawing techniques that
make their jobs effortless. So, with the grid technique,
beginner and intermediate Celtic designers can easily
create or recreate advanced and complex drawings
efficiently in record time. For example, you may
experience some difficulties trying to draw a complex
Celtic knot. But, with the grid technique, you can

break down the knot into smaller manageable segments. Next, you focus on replicating what's in each segment on your drawing paper. Still, grid technique aids speedy completion of great drawing projects. It can help you run many designs in record time and earn higher income.

Using the Grid Technique to Scale Drawings

Use the grid technique to transpose images in a piece of paper to another one. Again, no special drawing ability is required from anyone to use this technique. Just explore these steps to attain great results.

Required Items

- The image to draw

- A scaled drawing paper

- A pencil

- An eraser

- A ruler

- A pen

Instructions

Follow these simple steps to scale your drawings with grid technique

1. Pick your image: Feel free to pick any Celtic knot, but, if you find drawing too difficult, or you haven't worked with the technique before, opt for a simple Celtic pattern.

2. Select your drawing paper: Scale the paper to the size of your image.

3. Mark the edges of the image: Make sure that the marks are evenly spaced.

4. Use a ruler to join opposite marks: Connect the lines to form a grid pattern.

5. Mark the edges of your paper: Again, make sure that the marks are evenly spaced and use your ruler to connect the opposite marks to create a grid pattern similar to the previous one. However, the grid lines and markings on the paper should be lightly drawn because you'll still need to erase them.

6. Assign numbers to each box on the image and paper: From the top-left corner, number each box so that you'll know the image to knit to each box on the drawing paper. Again, press your pencil lightly on the drawing paper because you'll still need to erase the assigned numbers.

7. Begin drawing: Recreate the content of the image on the drawing paper box-by-box. Feel free to start with any box but make sure the

selected image goes to the appropriate box on
the drawing paper. Use your pencil to draw
throughout because you might have to adjust
the drawings.

8. Erase the grid and numbers: Allow the ink to
    dry completely before you clean the grid and
    numbers with your eraser.

9. Color the drawing: Feel free to use your
    favorite color.Yes, you need to decide on the
    color you want to use. Two or more colors may
    be used on the drawing but always make sure
    that you're comfortable with the color for the
    pattern.

Always focus on the image you are trying to create
so that you don't get lost in the process.

Chapter Summary

- Grid drawing technique can help you to attain
  accuracy when you are creating your sketches.

- Consider the shape and size of your pattern
  before you draw it before you use the grid
  technique to sketch it.

- Grid drawing helps you to focus on a particular
  section of an image or pattern at a time.

In the next chapter you will learn how to design your own Celtic pattern in the comfort of your home. See you there!↓

Chapter Five:
How to Design Your Own Celtic Pattern

You have traced so many drawn patterns on graph papers. Now, you need to go a step further by learning to draw or create Celtic patterns from scratch. Just follow the time-tested steps below to create great Celtic patterns in the comfort of your home.

Required Materials

- Graph paper

- A pencil

- A pen or marker

- An eraser

- Contrasting color marker

Instructions

Follow these steps to draw your own Celtic pattern.

2. Draw your grid: Create a few lines and columns on a staggered grid. Each column and row should be two squares apart but make sure they share the edges. Just count the dots on the

outside edges to now calculate your columns and rows. Also, feel free to vary the number of your columns and rows, but they must be even numbers. Mark dots in the middle of all your grids. Again, use another colored pen to mark dots on the sides of your grids.

3. Sketch a few vertical and horizontal lines: Create a few vertical and horizontal lines on your grid. Make sure that each line covers an even number of columns and rows, while the dot stays in the center of the line. Creativity is required here. So, feel free to up your creative ingenuity to create something amazing and attractive.

4. Connect the dots: Connect the unused dots with diagonal lines but don't join any of the vertical or horizontal lines yet. Next, draw a small arc between the vertical and horizontal lines and the already connected dots. Carefully evaluate how the dots fit into the lines and make sure that four lines are connected to each dot. Join alternating dots to close visible gaps on the pattern. Feel free to use a pen or a marker but you might want to use a pencil because you might make some errors or need to erase some dots or lines.

5. Draw the break lines: A break is a plain weaving design and it enhances the aesthetic layout of the Celtic pattern. Again, break lines

are like barriers embedded into a Celtic pattern to create a super exciting effect. Each break line could be as long as one square in the grid. The few chords that go with these lines must not cross the lines in the pattern. Turn these cords away from the lines to create a closed loop of beautiful patterns. So, how do I include break lines in my Celtic pattern?

a. Be mindful of how you do it because break lines could be wrongly added to a pattern and the whole thing will be messed up. No! Don't be discouraged. You can experiment with it as long as you want but I will give you two simple tips on how to create amazing break lines. Again, the tips will help you save time, effort, and paper, and also come up with an authentic and beautiful pattern. Here are the tips:

b. Position the break line on the edge of each square, directly on the grid line, but make sure that the line starts and stops between the grid lines.

c. Position the break line in the center of each square, between the grid lines, but make sure it starts and stops at the next grid line.

d. There is no fixed rule on how to sketch the break line. It all depends on what you want your pattern to look like. For example, you could sketch your break line downward from the top to create separate sections within the pattern. So, take your time to study the pattern you want to create and tailor your break lines accordingly. Still, you may want to connect two break lines to create certain aesthetic effects. No worries. Create one break line on the edge of a square while the other stays in-between. Don't be tempted to burden your pattern with too many breaks. Repeat your pattern of breaks at reasonable intervals to create an enticing effect. Use a pencil to draw the break lines and don't forget to keep the curves smooth and enticing.

6. Add the curved lines: Stylishly connect the curved lines to the break lines. Here are the techniques to use in drawing smooth curved lines.

    a. Do a 5-minute session of drawing curves for about a week to master free-flow curved lines.

    b. Practice with images similar to the pattern you want to draw. Try to redesign the reference images accurately. Don't be in a hurry - you won't increase your level of expertise until you have done it over and over again. Remember the goal here is to draw an amazing and original pattern you could call your own. Learn new patterns to upgrade your drawing skills and style.

c. Work on a different pattern. See how you can replicate the pattern on your own. You could use the skills you learned while copying previous images but let your own skills begin to evolve. Study the new pattern and structure out a plan to redesign it your own way. Again, feel free to alter a few things about the pattern to make it more charming and attractive. Opt for interesting textures to stay motivated throughout the whole process.

d. Stylishly change the direction of your curves. Curves can be changed quarter-way, half-way, or third-way. Still, the direction of curves depends on the pattern you want to create.

e. Carefully consider the look of the curves before you start to sketch them. Again, be sure nothing disturbs or disrupts easy movement of your arms while you draw the curves. Why? You can't take a break when you are drawing curves.

f. Move your arm faster to draw neat and smooth curves. Fast movement of arms means you'll have minimal control over the curves at first but you'll eventually come up with great and confident lines.

g. Calm your shoulder muscles when you are drawing curves. Tense arms always come up with crooked and tense lines.

h. Consider the direction of your curves. Already, you know that curves play significant roles in the final outlook of a Celtic pattern. So, make sure you turn the curves to the objects they are meant to describe. It's one hard step you'll need to practice consistently to learn how to do it accurately.

7. Decide the shape of your Celtic pattern: Take your time to consider the intended outlook of your pattern to know whether you are still on track. Find out what was wrong with the earlier steps if you realize some things are out of place. However, should everything be in the right shape, create a basic outline on the pattern and fill the negative or empty spaces you come across there.

8. Join break and curved lines: Stylishly connect the break and curved lines to create an outstanding effect on the Celtic pattern.

9. Add finishing touches: Erase the outline and unused dots or lines carefully so that you don't mess things up. Again, feel free to use your favorite color to embellish the pattern.

Now you have completed your very first Celtic pattern. Congratulations! Use the secrets already learned to create different sizes of Celtic patterns.

Chapter Summary

- Make sure your columns and rows are two squares apart when you are designing a Celtic pattern.

- Don't burden your pattern with too many breaks if you don't want to mess it up.

In the next chapter you will learn how to create a Celtic maze pattern.↓

Chapter Six:
Celtic Maze Pattern and Game

Celtic maze patterns are straight spiral lines often used to connect dots. Remember that you connected a few dots when I took you through the process of making some unique Celtic designs. Good! Celtic maze patterns, however, are not that easy. You need to constantly practice how to design the patterns to master them. Do some pre-planning before you try to execute large projects so that you don't mess up the whole thing.

Don't fret because I am going to show you how to draw a Celtic maze pattern straight away. Still, in this chapter, you will also learn several amazing geometric drawing patterns and how to use them to beautify your Celtic artwork. First, let's quickly learn how to draw a Celtic maze pattern.

Required Materials

- A pen

- Some pieces of paper

- Creativity

Instructions

Follow these simple steps to make your Celtic maze pattern:

1. Draw the base shape of your design. To get it right, take your time to examine the pattern you want to create.

2. Sketch internal lines. Carefully add the inner shapes, circles, and other reference lines into the base shape but make sure you harmonize everything.

3. Add a break line. I have already shown you how to handle break lines. Just sketch the break lines on the base lines.

4. Replace the reference lines with curves.

5. Run this pattern on 3 more sides and connect them all together. You'll need to draw a maze-look-alike spiral knot to connect the sides, while the center will have a circular maze pattern.

6. Fill negative space with more patterns and knots.

Great! You have just designed your Celtic maze pattern.

Amazing Geometric Drawing Patterns for Celtic Projects

Shapes such as squares, triangles, and circles are fundamental to all images and designs, including Celtic knots, and they evoke varied meanings. For example, quilters and other drawing experts often use rectangles and squares to represent balance; triangles for energy and stability; hexagon for unity; and circles for protection. Still, these shapes provide perfect aesthetics for Celtic projects. Here, I will give you an array of shapes to create cohesive designs, and also show you how to use these shapes.

Patterns: You already know the importance of patterns in Celtic artwork. So, take your time to create lovely images with patterns. Even a simple shape looks appealing. You can imagine the beauty of a whole image of different shapes. You should carefully select the shapes you need to create a spectacular image landscape. Examine your project and the message you intend before you choose what patterns to use. Again, balance things up. Don't overlap your Celtic artwork with multiple patterns.

1. Patterns with photos: Consider splicing your photos into some patterns to create a striking effect. Paste a few photos of your Celtic knots in some shapes and experience its uniqueness. Shapes personalize images and make them stand out.

2. Lighting and shadows: Feel free to add lighting and shadow effects to your Celtic projects. Create a 3D design and use lighting and shadows to draw attention to particular sections of the Celtic artwork but you need creativity to make it unique. Remember that your level of creativity determines the beauty of your Celtic maze patterns, as well as other Celtic projects.

3. Collage: A collage of different shapes can enhance the aesthetics of your Celtic patterns and make them easy to view on screen. So, create these shapes within your Celtic pattern, and see how your artwork gets massive attention.

4. Diagonals: Use diagonals to help the eye trace your Celtic patterns. Focus on using diagonals to juxtapose the images and colors of your Celtic pattern. In other words, diagonals enhance the aesthetics of your artworks and make them appealing.

5. Isometric patterns: Use the three dimensional isometric patterns to highlight the uniqueness of your Celtic projects. Opt for a hard color if you want to create a striking effect when the image pops up on screen. However, be creative with isometric patterns because it could draw instant and sharp attention to certain words, items, or sections in your design.

6. Patterns with fonts: Combine patterns and typeface to stretch your creativity a bit and move your design capability to another level. Feel free to use different shapes and lines to make your design a little bit edgy or jagged.

7. Patterns within patterns: Sure, your Celtic pattern already has a few shapes. Fine. Consider adding more small shapes within the shapes to make them look complex and beautiful. Feel free to alternate the varieties of shapes for your design but make sure everything is harmonized.

8. Create a theme: Patterns can boost the beauty of Celtic knots. The outlook is better when you connect images to these patterns. It is amazing when the patterns complement one another. So, create a theme for your Celtic pattern. Make sure the images connect well with the borders, colors, and patterns. Create a design that easily becomes your trademark, one that can captivate the most vague minds.

9. Gradients: A cool color design attracts everyone. Don't just go for any color. Use a color that adds value to your artwork. Sure, a gradient background for your Celtic designs will boost its look. Carefully blend shapes together to make your artwork stand out. Still, opt for simplicity. Don't overuse color just

because you want to up the aesthetics of your design. It will mess up the whole thing.

10. Combine many images: Use shapes to mix some images in your Celtic artworks to form collages. See how the images spices up your design and how the shapes complement one another. Still, use only images that are relevant to the Celtic pattern you want to draw.

11. Create overlapping shapes: Feel free to overlap some shapes in your Celtic artwork to create some striking effects. Such shapes could catch the attention of everyone who sees your pattern. Experiment with overlapping shapes in a few Celtic designs and see the beauty such shapes could add to your designs.

12. Harmonize your colors: Opt for compatible colors to balance your Celtic knots. Avoid color riot. Feel free to select any color you want but make sure it is suitable for the pattern. For example, use an orange and deep green color mixture for serious and professional Celtic artworks. A poor color combination will put everyone off your design. Better still, consider how a few colors react together before you mix them for Celtic projects.

13. Make it subtle: Begin to use subtle shapes to adorn or beautify your Celtic artworks. Subtle shapes are not obvious. They work wonders by creating great aesthetic effects in drawings,

paintings, embroideries, and other artworks. Blend a few shapes into the design background to creatively turn your design to a cynosure of all eyes.

14. Do some hands-on patterns: Learn to go traditional by creating personalized hand-drawn patterns. Sure it's hard and time consuming but it's also appealing.

15. Use rare shapes: Do standout designs by using rare shapes and patterns. Don't be compelled to use regular squares, circles, or triangles to design your Celtic artwork. Use shapes that are totally new in the field of designing. Still, the shapes must be suitable for the Celtic knot you want to create.

16. Reduce complex patterns: Don't be tempted to overladen your Celtic artwork with complex patterns. Sure, these patterns add significant beauty to the artwork but they can also trigger loss of attraction. So, know why and when to use them to sustain viewers' attention. Better still, make sure that the complex patterns deserve their place before you use them.

17. Black and white pattern: Some patterns are just great when they appear in black and white, not colored. Also, black-and-white patterns are natural and appealing. So, rather than focusing on colored Celtic patterns all the time, do some

black-and-white natural patterns, and see how charming and appealing they really are.

Don't litter your Celtic artwork with so many patterns. You don't have to bore people with patterns, just because you want to highlight your project with fancy designs. Remember that these patterns can lose their impact when you overuse them. Therefore, carefully consider what your Celtic knot really needs to be charming and appealing. Again, it's up to you to take your Celtic designs to a greater height.

Chapter Summary

- Celtic maze patterns are spiral lines used to connect dots.

- Constant practice can enhance the designs of great Celtic maze patterns.

- Examine your project and the message you want to portray before you choose any pattern.

Chapter Seven captures the special features of medieval illuminated manuscripts and how you can create one.↓

Chapter Seven:
Medieval Illuminated Manuscript

There was an increase in the demand for illuminated manuscripts in European and Arab nations during the Middle Ages. Then, they used beautiful materials such as vellum, silverpoint, and gold leaf to beautify or illuminate the pages of books and manuscripts. Since there were no sewing or quilting machines at that time, the process of illustrating, gilding, or writing the manuscript was done by hand. You need to exhibit a high degree of craftsmanship. Many illuminated manuscripts didn't survive because of the quality of the materials used to design them and the incessant wars in medieval Europe. Those that made it to our present world are treasured, and they expose the customs and practices of the Middle Ages people to us.

Initials of kingdoms sending a message were showcased via illuminated manuscript scrolls in the Medieval period. In this chapter, you will learn how to design or create illuminated manuscripts.

We will write a letter 'A.' All letters share the same concept. Just try to visualize what each letter looks like and adopt the concept of drawing here to create any letter you want. Good. Here's how to create the letter 'A.'

Required Materials

- Cotton paper (hot pressed)

- White gel pen

- A pen

- A ruler

- Pencil and eraser

Instructions

Follow these simple steps to create your own letter 'A.'

1. Draw a grid with a ruler.

2. Use a pencil and ruler to sketch a rough outline of the letter 'A' on the grid.

3. Sketch the letter's confinement box and use your pen to add details of letter 'A' inside the confinement.

4. Highlight the box and letter outlines, and erase the pencil marks.

5. Design the letter in the box and shade with your pencil.

6. Add your favorite color, and highlight the letter with the white gel.

Congratulations. You just designed your own letter 'A' for a medieval illuminated manuscript.

How to Make Illuminated Manuscripts

Writing and painting were done by hand during the Middle Ages, but, as of the 12th century, illustrators began to illuminate their paintings on thin sheets of valuable metals, and this aided the popularity of illuminated manuscripts. The whole process was very stressful in those days but it is great fun today! An afternoon's work is enough to create a story and design it with charming images in the pattern of the medieval illuminated manuscripts. How am I going to do it? No worries because here is how.

Writing the Text

Ready 15 or 20 pieces of thick, white parchment. Cut each piece to 8" by 11" but feel free to decide what is enough for your manuscript. Different types of parchment are readily available in virtually all paper supply stores. Still, opt for parchments that are dusted with pumice powder because their surfaces are rough and receptive to paint and ink. But, should you find no parchment, opt for thick and white cardstocks.

Trim the end of your quill or you won't be able to write with it. Traditionally, the Middle Ages people used feather quills from chickens, ducks, or geese to write text on their illuminated manuscripts. Just get a dried quill from any of these animals, use your scissors to trim the tip a bit to make it pointed, and write with it. Quills are readily available in paper supply stores but feel free to use a fountain pen if you can't get a quill.

Ready a small bowl of black ink, dip the quill's tip into the ink, shake off excess ink from the quill, and start writing your letters on the manuscript. But, if black ink isn't your favorite ink for the project, use the ink you like.

Select the pages you want to write on. Freely write in the top, middle, or bottom portion of the pages you select, or you could just reserve the whole page for images. Again, feel free to create borders around the edges of the pages or draw out where you'll place your drawn pictures. Remember that traditional manuscripts had many large images and fewer words per page. Again, pay keen attention to the first letter on each page to make it larger and more detailed than other letters within the page.

Create your own story or copy one from the Middle Ages. Just make sure that the story you are using depicts fanciful events and heroic achievements. Write the text a few times on a scrap paper to master it. Then, write it on your manuscript. Use calligraphy or some old-fashioned decorative writing aids to create your text and make sure the whole thing appears neat and fancy.

Spread out the manuscript to dry the ink. Usually, black inks on parchment paper can take up to 15 minutes to dry. Let the whole thing dry completely before you move on to the next stage. Also, while quilling the text, keep your hands off the paper or you'll smudge the ink.

Adding Images and Designs

Use the quill and ink to draw your images and designs. Just make sure you mark out your design to know where to fit in the color on the page. Add a few sketches of the scenes of your story and charming images to spice up the manuscript, but allow the ink to dry completely for about 10 minutes before adding new colors. Don't forget that classic illuminated manuscripts had 2D images of fanciful tales as themes, but feel free to create your favorite theme designs.

Sketch a border around your text. The style depends on the look you want to give your illuminated manuscript. Just make sure that the borders are fanciful. Use the quill and black ink to sketch a few flowers, leaves, or vines round the edges of the page to make your manuscript attractive and charming.

Create a base coat for gold leaf, attach a small paint brush to it, press it on your favorite areas on the page, and carefully paint the coat base on the paper. Plasters are used to make base coats and you can get the coats in any of the craft supply stores out there. Feel free to brush excess gold leaf off the page, but you'll have to use a fluffy paint brush to do it. Do you know about gold leaf? It is actually a thin layer of real

real gold, and you can use a paint brush to manipulate it to add majestic lighting to your favorite images.

Use watercolor paints to color your design. Decide the colors to use for the whole image. Dab color to the areas you want to highlight with a paint brush but don't continue the remaining areas until the paint dries off completely. If you are working on this project with your kids, allow them to fill the images with bright-colored paints or glitter glue. Focus on using deep reds, purples, or light greens because they illuminate manuscripts more than other colors. Also, consider using tan or white paint to highlight other objects and figures.

Binding the Pages

Arrange the pages in the right order, cut them to equal sizes, but make sure nothing is missing from the text. Get the left sides of the pages arranged in 3 narrow leather thongs. Spread the thongs across the pages of your book to firmly hold the manuscript. Leather thongs are readily available in craft supply stores but feel free to use synthetic thongs if you can't get leather thongs.

Use lined thread to sew the pages to the thongs. How do I go about this? Pass a thick linen thread through your needle, knot it the end, sew the top of the pages with your leather thongs, and attach all the pages, one after the other, but in a straight line. Doing this can be difficult if your manuscript has too many pages, but you can work one section at a time.

Use wooden boards to loop the leather thongs. Ready two wooden boards but make sure they are larger than your already cut-out pages. Arrange the thongs on the boards, mark their end points, pop out 3 holes with a chisel, pull out the thongs via the holes, and tie them. Use your scissors to cut off excess leather from the book.

Use as much gold leaf as possible and spice up your images with creativity. Again, images on illuminated manuscripts are not always perfect pictures. Just exercise caution if you are using bookbinding tools for the project since they can be tricky to use.

Here are the materials you'll need to do this project.

- 16 to 20 pieces of parchment

- Quill

- Black ink

- Watercolors

- Gold leaf

- Base coat

- Paint brush

- Leather thongs

- Sewing needle

- Chisel

- 2 wooden boards

- Linen thread

Take a bold step to create and illuminate your initials. Just ready some colored pencils, gold crayons, black-felt tip pen, an animated pet or plant, and an 18 cm by 18 cm square piece of paper to get started.

Chapter Summary

- Demand for illuminated manuscripts was high in European and Arab Nations during the Middle Ages.

- Many illuminated manuscripts did not survive at the time because of the quality of the materials and the incessant wars of the period.

In the next chapter, I will take you around the world of Celtic symbols.↓

Chapter Eight: Celtic Symbols

Celtic patterns are bold, adorable, and appealing but they all have their unique meanings. Each Celtic symbol has a particular message. Today, we will go back in history to carefully study their meanings. So, sit comfortably and relax, while I take you around the world of Celtic symbols.

Celtic Knots

Triquetra

Triquetra is also known as the trinity knot. It is the symbol of the Mother, Maiden, and Crone, a neo-pagan goddess. It uses the moon to showcase the circles of a woman's life. It also symbolizes the three circles of life— life, death, and rebirth; the marital vows of the husband to his wife—love, honor, and protection; the phases of time—past, present, and future; or the family structure—father, mother, and children.

Recently, Christians started using it to propagate 'The Father, The Son, and The Holy Spirit' aspect of faith. Irish jewelry designers regularly incorporate Triquetra into their jewelry pieces to symbolize everlasting love and Irish ancestry.

Square Knot

Square knot is also the shield knot and it has elaborate and complex meanings. It may symbolize the elements of nature—earth, wind, fire, and water; the St. Brigid's four tiers of wisdom—heart, head, hearth, and hand; or the four unique Celtic festivals—Imbolic, Samhain, Lughnasadh, and Bealtaine. Still, the square knot can also symbolize good fortune, prosperity, and protection against witchcraft.

Circular Knot

Circular knots come in different forms and they symbolize purity and wholeness. For example, the five fold symbol, a modern circular knot, has an unseen element which connotes religion. Celts are very religious. Dara knot is another example of a circular knot. 'Doire' is the Irish word for Dara and it means 'oak tree.' Oaks are sacred trees in Celtic culture because they symbolize leadership, power, wisdom, and strength.

Spirals

Single

The single spiral is a common Celtic symbol seen on monuments and other artifacts. It could symbolize growth, balance, progress, connection, and direction. Again, depending on how one uses it, the single spiral could mean a journey from the material world to the cosmic world or the expansion of consciousness, learning, and experiences.

Double

A clockwise movement of two points on a line forms the double spiral and, like the single spiral, it has varied meanings. It is often used to symbolize the sun and its double spiral movement over a year. It may represent balance while one runs two opposing activities at the same time. It may also mean a spiritual symbol of awakening, creation and destruction, or birth and death.

Triple

The triple spiral is an ancient Celtic symbol. It became very popular in 500 BC and its meanings depend on how it is used. It could symbolize motion, energy, progress, cycles, or revolution. Also, the three arms of the spiral can connote, spirit, mind, and body; life, death, and rebirth; father, mother, and children; power, intellect, and love; past, present, and future; or creation, preservation, and destruction, depending on the culture of the place where the triple spiral is used. Still, the triple spiral could symbolize the spiritual, physical, and celestial worlds.

Animal and Trees

Birch and Stag

Birch trees are unique in the Celtic mythology. They can symbolize grace, purity, connections, healing, protection, femininity, and new life. Celts often see the tree as a goddess and they believe that the white bark of the tree could protect people from evil and spiritual attacks. Stag, on the other hand, symbolizes the forest, and it produces antlers, similar to the branches of a tree. It may also mean the deer animal symbol. For the birch people, stag is a male animal symbol, while deer is for the female animal.

Stag often symbolizes empathy, intuition, and extrasensory perception. Stag is a symbol for nature since it is strong, fast, sexually vigorous, and agile. It is believed that birch and stag could boost a person's quality of life. Still, ancient history held that birch trees could protect people from lightning.

So, what's your next birthday? The birch tree is your astrology sign if your birthday falls between 24th December and 21st January. Do you know what this means? People with the astrology sign are movers, risk takers, achievers, passionate, strategists, and innovators.

Rowan and Cat

The rowan tree has many meanings. It is the zodiac sign for people whose birthdays fall between

January 21 and February 17. Such people, according to Celtic culture, are great thinkers. Again, it is widely held that the tree can give humans energy to be creative and original in every task, as well as the capacity to stay positive throughout one's earthly journey. Also, the tree could symbolize death and rebirth if used in funeral rites or protection if placed at gates and doorways. Still, it is a symbol of great blessings, protection, and unwavering insights. So, when something threatens or challenges you, learn to trust your guts and instincts.

Congratulations if your birthday falls under the rowan tree astrological sign. Just know that your attributes will be reinforced by the cat, your animal symbol, and you have nine lives. Still, when people fail to make an impact, you will record great success. Again, your animal symbol makes you fiercely independent and self-reliant but you'll exhibit some forms of mischievousness.

Ash and Snake

The ash tree is a symbol of how the three worlds connect—underworld, earth, and spiritual world. Feel free to call it Tree or Worlds or World Tree. Still, it symbolizes the three phases of time—past, present, and future, as well as protection, greater heights, expansion, and growth. The ash tree is the astrological sign of people whose birthday falls between February 18 and March 17. Although such people are very protective, they have enchanting and endearing personalities. Nion or Nun, the alphabet that represents the ash tree, symbolizes a person's unhindered ability to travel around the three worlds. So, your animal symbol is the snake.

The snake is the Celts' symbol of health and rebirth. It sees beyond the veil that separates the three worlds from one another and it is a source of intuition and uncanny capacity to see beyond difficulties.

Alder and Fox

Alder symbolizes originality and insight. Anyone whose birthday falls between March 18 and April 14 has the alder zodiac sign. The alder tree breeds self-confidence and self-trust and this explains why people with the alder zodiac sign are trailblazers. So, if you fall under this zodiac sign, begin to focus more on the fox, your animal symbol. The fox is so clever and cunning that people or other animals hardly outsmart it.

Willow and Cow

The willow tree symbolizes one who observes life and everything in it. It breeds strength and unwavering determination to overcome obstacles and challenges on the path of one's success. People whose birthday falls between April 15 and May 12 have the willow zodiac sign and they exhibit strong will-power. Should you fall under the willow zodiac sign, your animal symbol is cow, a stubborn and loyal animal. So, as you stay loyal to your goals, you're stubborn enough to face challenges that pop up on the way to your breakthrough.

Hawthorn and Seahorse

The hawthorn tree has good and bad meanings. The thorny crown on Jesus Christ's head before his crucifixion is obtained from the hawthorn tree. The sign is interpreted based on the circumstances of the moment but the tree is usually a symbol of freedom. Hawthorn is your astrological sign if your birthday is between May 13 and June 9. Still, the tree stands for fertility and protection from evil or harm. So, just as your seahorse, your animal symbol, can maneuver the sea despite its high torrents and current, you have the strength to turn difficulties into opportunities. It is widely believed that the seahorse could help you with financial acumen and infallible memory.

Oak and Wren

The oak tree is very significant to the Celts. The Celts say the tree can motivate you to attain greater heights while the Druids see it as a sacred emblem of existence. These people use the tree for wealth and durability spells. Your astrological sign is oak if your birthday falls between June 10 and July 7, and your animal symbol is wren. The oath tree could breed strength and self-reliance. So, just like wren, your animal symbol, you should be industrious, focused, and fortified with strength.

Holly and Horse

The holly tree symbolizes legacy, immortality, prestige, and royalty. It applies to people who are born between July 8 and August 4, and such people found grace with highly dignified personalities. Celts say that holly boughs can ward off evil spirits simply by using them to decorate doorways and gates. Again, many years back, people cut branches off the trees during the winter period and kept them in their houses to provide shelter for fairies, just because they thought holly trees housed fairies. If you fall under the zodiac sign of the holly tree, your animal symbol is horse. Like the horse, believe in your power, stamina, willpower and stubbornness, and make sure you are attaining your goals.

Hazel and Salmon

The hazel tree stands for wisdom, knowledge, and the willpower to attain goals despite the challenges of life. Knowledge here covers formal education and innate intuitiveness. The tree is more about magic wells and springs, and it centers on the universal energy on which all life thrives. Anyone whose birthday is between August 5 and September 1 falls under the zodiac sign of the hazel tree. Salmon, your animal symbol, can go all the way to achieve its goals despite difficult challenges. You, like other hazel tree people, should exhibit this type of commitment.

Vine and Swan

The vine tree stands for balance and people born between September 2 and September 29 always strive to balance things up to make life good for everyone. Remember that balance and harmony work hand-in-hand. So, people with the zodiac sign of the vine tree often develop the gift of prophecy and are unrepentant truth-speakers. Like swan, your animal symbol, don't falter or stop on the path of your goals when obstacles or challenges pile up.

Ivy and Butterfly

The ivy plant grows one step at a time like a baby who's learning to crawl. Anyone whose birthday falls between September 30 and October 27 has the zodiac sign of the ivy tree. Such people rarely take risks unless they are sure things will go their way. Once they make a move, they focus their goals until they achieve them. Know that your animal symbol is the butterfly, known for its survival and transformation. Like the animal symbol, people with the ivy zodiac sign tend to live light-hearted and carefree lifestyles but they always endure life's hardships and challenges.

Reed and Wolf

Anyone whose birthday falls between October 28 and November 4 has the reed zodiac sign and they are versatile in everything they do. Such people have the capacity to refine raw things and make them useful.

They are talented and would surely do well in skill-based careers. It is widely held that the reed plant breeds healing and helps one to build strong ties towards one's family. However, the wolf, your animal symbol, is known for its power, independence, and self-confidence, the same characteristics you need to develop.

Elder and Falcon

The elder tree is also known as the judgment tree. It applies to people who fall under the zodiac sign of the elder tree. The birthday of such people is between November 5 and December 23 and they often end up as judges and jurists. Such people try to remain fair and balanced in everything they do. Again, their passion and desire for justice is innate and they are always willing to render services to other people.

So, if elder is your astrological sign, always remember the falcon or hawk, your animal symbol. Soar higher and aim for greater heights because you have the capacity to see things far ahead of other people. Celtic mythology believes that the falcon could provide direction to people with the elder sign towards achieving their life's goals and pursuits.

Chapter Summary

- Triquetra, also known as the trinity knot, could symbolize life, death, and rebirth of love, honor, and protection.

- Square knot may also symbolize the natural elements of the universe such as Earth, wind, fire, and water.

Next, we will take a look at zoomorphic knotwork animals. See you there!↓

Chapter Nine:
Zoomorphic Knotwork Animals

Celtic artworks are not limited to knots and braids. No. Animals with bodies, limbs, tails, and tongues form a critical part of the Celtic culture. It is little wonder that illuminated manuscripts of the Middle Ages were decorated with birds, dogs, dragons, and all sorts of animals. Ancient books, like the Book of Kells, were illuminated with dazzling and inspiring zoomorphic images and designs, and people still find these books interesting and fulfilling. Almost all jewelry of the period was embellished with beasts and birds. Bestiaries, books on animals, showcased the natural symbolism of animals in the Middle Ages and their supposed spiritual meanings. These books tend to describe the interactions of medieval Europeans with domestic and wild animals, as well as mythical creatures such as unicorns and griffins.

Common zoomorphic animals in medieval Celtic artworks included quadrupeds, birds, and serpents. Dogs and lions were the most designed quadrupeds of the period. But, since the style used in designing these quadrupeds was highly abstract, it is hard to tell which one was a dog or a lion. However, lions and dogs have their personal symbolic attributes. A dog is loyal to its owner and its tongue has some healing powers. Lions symbolize royalty, pride, and strength.

A lion is always vigilant and awake, even when it is sleeping.

Eagles and peacocks are the most designed birds during the Middle Ages. These birds have symbolic meanings in the Celtic tradition. Eagles, for example, symbolize royalty and they are respected for their strength and acute vision. Celtic mythology holds that an eagle is bound to experience an impaired vision when it grows old. Even at that, it gets a renewed strength to fly higher close to the sun. When it eventually gets there, its vision is restored. Again, Celts believed that peacocks have immortal flesh. For them, when peacocks die, their bodies do not decay. So, peacocks became a symbol of everlasting life for the Celtic people.

Snakes and serpents too are amazing zoomorphic knotwork animals. Carefully consider their natural and attractive slender bodies. Again, contorting them into Celtic knots and spirals is quite easy. Snakes could be a good or bad symbol. Remember the event in the garden of Eden. Satan disguised himself as a serpent to tempt Eve. Also, the shedding of the skin of a snake could also symbolize spiritual cleansing or salvation. Ancient legends, beliefs, and the culture of the Celtic people focused on the symbolic meanings of zoomorphic designs.

In this chapter, I will be sharing Celtic myths on the most commonly designed zoomorphic knotwork animals. First, I will take you through the process of integrating a bird knot into your Celtic artwork. Just follow these steps to do it.

Required Materials

- Pencil

- Scale

Instructions

Follow these simple steps to integrate zoomorphic knotwork animals into your Celtic artwork.

1. Use the pencil and scale to sketch a rectangle of 12 cm by 4.5 cm.

2. Sketch a vertical line in the center of the rectangle's longer side.

3. Draw a cross in the middle of the vertical line, 0.5 cm away from the top, to create a block.

4. Sketch the pattern of the zoomorphic knotwork animal on the left and right sides of the block.

    a. Feel free to use a tracing paper if you can't sketch the pattern directly into the artwork. Still, make sure that you use feather-like hands to draw the pattern. Highlight the edges with a water-gel black pen.

b. Don't try to overlap two highlight lines just because you want to balance things up. You may only overlap breaks.

5. Erase rough drawings or pencil lines after you complete highlighting the edges.

6. Add other details into the pattern with your pen.

7. Use light strokes for light highlights or heavy strokes for dark ones.

Congratulations. You just made a Celtic bird knot.

Celtic Myths on Selected Zoomorphic Knotwork Animals

Each zoomorphic knotwork animal had its story and meaning in the Celtic mythology. Some of these myths sound funny or bizarre but the Medieval people attach significant meanings to animals. Here, I will share mystical stories of some of these animals with you.

Celtic Wolf: Wolf was a respected animal in Celtic culture. It was widely believed that wolves nursed one of the most popular kings in ancient Ireland.

Celtic Eagle: Lleu Llaw Gyffes was a legend in Wales. When grown, his wife's lover struck him with a spear, and Lleu turned into an eagle and attempted to fly away to distant lands. But Gwydion, Lleu's foster father and uncle, tracked him down to an oak tree, where Lleu was perching.

Celtic Owl: Gwydion found Lleu and transformed him to his human form. He also transformed Blodeuwedd, Lleu's unfaithful wife, to an owl. Other birds hated her and she had to live or fly in the night. Owls do not come out in broad daylight.

Celtic Boar: The Boar of Benn Gulbain had killed 50 of Finn Mac's men. So, Finn prepared to kill the wild boar to avenge the death of his men. Finn and his men, while trying to hunt the animal, got to a hilltop, where they met Diarmait, but Finn's men ran away when the wild animal was fast approaching. Diarmait stayed behind, killed the boar, and also died there because a curse was on him from childhood to die the day he hunts or kills a boar.

Celtic Salmon: The Salmon of Knowledge went down into the Well of Wisdom to eat up nine hazelnuts that fell into the well. The poet Finegas tried to fish out the Salmon for seven years. When he finally caught it, he told Finn Mac Cool to cook it. However, he warned Finn not to eat any part of the Salmon. Still, Finn placed his thumb on the fish to test if it was thoroughly cooked, and he burned his thumb in the process. Immediately Finn's thumb reached his mouth, Finn obtained the wisdom of the Salmon.

Celtic Raven: The Raven is the symbol of Morrigan, the Celtic Goddess of War, Fate, and Death.

Celts people believe that the goddess determines who would live or die in the battlefield.

Celtic Stag: Deer is the symbol of Cernunnos, the Celtic god of fertility, wealth, animals, life, and the underworld.

Celtic Hare: Osin, a popular Celtic warrior, hunted down a hare and wounded its leg. He tried to approach the animal but saw a door opening on the ground. The door led him into a large hall where a beautiful young woman sat on a throne. The woman had a fresh wound in her leg and she was bleeding.

Celtic Bull: Medb, the Connacht queen, and Ailill, her husband, wanted to steal Donn Cuailnge, the stud bull, in the legendary Cattle Raid of Cooley in Ulster. Cú Chulainn, a teenager, eventually opposed them.

Celtic Bear: Artio was a Celtic Goddess. Celts people portrayed her as a bear and a woman. Also, Arthur of Camelot, the popular warrior-king, was closely linked to the bear. Many Celtic families had their personal animal totem during the Middle Ages.

Celtic Swans: Have you read the myth Children of Lir? Lir got married to Aoibh and she had four children by him. Eventually, Aoibh died and her sister, Aoife married her husband. Lir and the children loved one another so much that Aoife began to feel jealousy. So, she ordered one of her servants to kill the four children but the servant refused. Aoife too could not kill the children but eventually transformed them to swans.

Celtic Horse: According to the Celtic folklore, the puca changes shape and form at will. It could transform into a black horse or a goat, and it often brought good or bad omen for people. Also, the Celtic horse symbolized the Goddess of Epona and Rhiannon.

Celtic Cranes: It was widely believed that three cranes guarded Midir Brí Léith's house, preventing unauthorized access.

Celtic Hind: Sadhbh refused to enter into a relationship withTuatha Dé Danann, a dark druid. Angered by her refusal, the druid cursed her by transforming her into a deer. She was later told that she would be free from her curse if she could set her feet in the dún of Fianna, Ireland. Finn Mac Cool eventually saw her. As soon as he entered Almhuin, her curse was lifted and she became her old self, a beautiful young woman. She later got married to Finn and soon became pregnant. Still, while Finn fought against the Vikings in distant lands, the dark druid disguised as Finn to trick Sadhbh out of the house and changed her to a deer again. For seven year, Finn searched for his wife but didn't find her. He later found Oisin, his young son.

Chapter Summary

- Birds, dogs, dragons, and other animals were critical to Celtic culture in the Middle Ages.

- These animals symbolized many things in the Ancient Celtic tradition. For example, Eagles symbolized royalty while the deer was considered as the Celts' god of fertility and the underworld.

In the next chapter you will learn how to create a double celtic knot paracord.

Chapter Ten:
Double Celtic Knot Paracord

Double Celtic knot paracord is appealing and enchanting, a unique gift for someone who's close to your heart. Design it as a bracelet or a necklace and its uniqueness will amaze you. In this chapter, I will show you how to design a stylish double Celtic knot paracord necklace and you're surely going to like it. The project is simple and fun, and you can make it in the comfort of your home.

Required Materials

- 2 pieces paracords (opt for your favorite color)

- Glue

- Fake ornaments

Instructions

Follow these simple steps to create your own double Celtic knot paracord necklace

1. Loop the left side of both paracords from middle to the back.

2. Fold the other side forward anticlockwise and increase the size of the right loop.

3. Pass the right loop from behind to the right one.

4. Run the ends of the right cords via the left negative space in the left loop.

5. Run the ends again from the front via the middle loop.

6. Pass the ends from behind to the left loop.

7. Pull the pair of ends firmly in the opposite direction.

8. Pass the 4 ends through an artificial diamond bit and cross-loop the two one-color cords.

9. Run the other 2 cords via the cross-looped cords to create another Celtic knot base.

10. Loosen the knot base a bit, pass its ends to the opposite knot via the loop of another color, and cut excess ends and color cord you don't need.

11. Use other cords for the lace of your pendent and stick your jewelry pendant in the center of the Celtic knot.

You just designed a unique double Celtic knot paracord necklace, congratulations.

How to Tie a Celtic Heart Knot Paracord

A Celtic heart knot paracord is an appealing gift of love. It has a dazzling effect on bracelets and necklaces, and you can create it right there in your home. Yes, the process of designing a Celtic heart knot paracord is quite simple. Okay, let me just show you how to create it.

1. Carefully fold the cord to design a simple loop like the heart.

2. Stretch the end of the right cord downward through the loop.

3. Push up the right cord end through the upper loop and relax it down through the lower loop.

4. Run the cord through the down loop while its end goes up through the middle loop and down through the loop at the top.

5. Pinch the knot to form a heart.

How to Tie an Emperor's Snake Knot

An Emperor's snake knot is rarely seen or used but it is charming and appealing. Still, it is one knot everyone wants to tie because of its uniqueness. So, expect to see lots of variations on how people tie it. Yes, that's originality in design. I'll soon show you how to tie the knot but feel free to use it as a standalone, or spice it up as keychains, bracelets, necklaces, or other designs that thrill you. Eager to tie an Emperor's snake knot? Good! Here's how to do it.

First, tie the normal snake knot, add two loops to its side to give it the loop of an Emperor knot. Still, like the regular snake knot, the Emperor's snake knot is a 2 stranded knot.

Instructions

Just follow these simple steps to tie your Emperor's snake knot.

1. Ready 2 strands and use the left end of the strands to create a loop.

2. Run the right end top-down from the loop before it passes behind the left end.

3. Stretch it back to the right loop to design the regular snake knot.

4. Run the right end top-down into the right loop through the back of the right strand.

5. Pass the left end top-down through the left loop close to the front of the left strand.

6. Run the slack to the two ends through the side loops and tighten it up.

Great work! Congratulations. You just learned how to tie an Emperor's snake knot.

What Size of Paracord Do I Need for My Celtic Knot?

Every Celtic project requires planning. Part of this planning is to know how much paracord you need for a particular project. Unfortunately, most guidebooks out there do not come with basic tips on how anyone can plan ahead for their paracord projects. Here, I shall be showing you the amount of paracords you'll need to design a few Celtic knot projects.

Paracord for Bracelets

Running out of cords in the middle of a project is annoying, but this can surely be dealt with. The standing rule for anyone who's designing a cobra weave or any other weave is that they should ready one foot of paracord for one inch of bracelet. Still, this rule may change if your wrists are very large or you intend to design a very wide bracelet. Also, don't forget to ready one and a half feet of paracord for your center strands. A perfect amount of paracord for most bracelets is 10 feet. Here is a rough sketch of the amount of paracord to have ready for 8" wrist bracelets.

- 8 to 10 ft. for cobra

- 8.5 ft. for spiral quick-release.

- 25 ft. for king cobra.

- 8 to 10 ft. for corkscrew or telephone cord.

- 16 to 20 ft. for trilobite.

Paracord for Belts

Belts are longer and wider than all bracelets. So, be prepared to ready tons of cords when you want to design one. Again, the amount of cords for belts depends on the size of your project. You'll need 120 ft. of paracord for a double Cobra belt.

Paracord for Handle Wraps

It is hard to give an estimate of cords to ready for handle wraps. Why? What to use depends on the length and diameter of the project and the method you plan to use. So, calculate the length and diameter of your handle to know the amount of paracord to order. However, to design a West Country Whipping with 1" handle diameter, you'll need 40" paracord per handle inch.

Paracord for Other Designs

Try to have extra paracord ready for complex projects because you will not always find suitable formulas for estimates. Here are some cordage estimates.

- 10 to 15 feet for turks head coaster

- 50 feet water bottle net with sling

- 7 feet leash

- 37 feet 4-strand round braid

How to Conserve Your Paracord

Earlier, I told you that the size of your design and the method you choose to adopt could determine how much paracord you'll use for the project. Still, you can conserve your paracord. How? Pay keen attention to the following tips.

1. Don't detach from the spool during the process of designing a cobra bracelet. Wait until you finish the bracelet if you want to conserve your paracord. So, how can I do this? Make your bracelet cord 4 or 5 feet and slack it at the end of your weaving line. Still, make sure that your standing end goes up when you are weaving. Do you know where the standing end is? Yes, it is the area joined to the spool. With this, you won't need to lift the spool while you're designing a knot.

2. Leave between 3 and 5 feet paracord to practice new knots.

3. Use leftover paracord pieces to design rings, zipper pulls, keychains, and similar designs.

4. Weave 3" projects with scrap pieces of paracord and divide what you used by 3 to know your average cord for one inch.

Still, these tips may not work for all projects because it is hard to estimate the amount of paracord required for all designs. And, most times, a trial-by-error approach is used to determine the pieces of paracord to ready for a project.

Chapter Summary

- A double Celtic knot paracord is a unique gift for someone who is very special to you.

- Carefully consider the size of the paracord you need for a particular project before you start it.

Chapter Eleven is all about Celtic monkey fist and how you can design one. See you there.↓

Chapter Eleven:
Celtic Monkey Fist

Celtic monkey fist is a charming ornamental knot. Many years ago, the Celtic monkey fist knot provided extra weight for the sailor's heaving line, making it easier for sailors to throw their cable to the shore. In this chapter, I will teach you how to design a Celtic monkey fist with or without a marble.

Required Materials

- A pair of scissors

- 4 ft. paracord

- Creativity

Instructions

Follow these simple steps to create your own Celtic monkey fist without marble.

1. Fold one end of your paracord, create a curve in the 'U' side of the cord, and run the end of the paracord through the curve.

2. Trim the excess to shorten the cord and place two fingers on the cord ball— top and down parts of the ball.

3. Muffle the cord twice on those fingers to create 2 curves, run the end of the cord thrice around the curves, and then carefully remove your fingers.

4. Circle the cord over the curves to design a circular curve on the ball and cut trim excess cord off.

Great work so far. You just designed a monkey fist without a marble. Let us move a bit further to design one with a marble.

How to Design a Monkey Fist with a Marble

A few minutes ago, you learned how to design a monkey fist without a marble. Now, I will teach you how to make one with a marble. Still, just like the previous fist, you can create this at the comfort of your home, although you could face some issues during your first few attempts. Here is how to design it.

Required Materials

- A pair of scissors

- Lighter

- 4 ft. paracord

- A marble

- A pointy object

- A bit of patience

Instructions

Follow these simple steps to create your monkey fist with a marble.

1. Fold one end of your paracord, create a loop in the 'U' side of the cord, run the end of the cord through the loop, trim to shorten the cord, and place two fingers on the cord ball— top and down parts.

2. Muffle the cord twice on your two fingers to create 2 loops, run the end of the cord thrice around the loops, and carefully loose your fingers. Circle the cord over the loops to create another circular loop on the ball.

3. Fix the marble in the center of the circular loop, tighten the cord slowly and gradually, and use the pointy object if it is hard to pull the cord.

You just finished making a monkey fist with a marble.

Monkey Fist Keychain

Feel free to design a monkeyfist keychain if you love creating amazing things from rope or paracord. A monkey fist keychain is easy and fun to design, and something you'll want to design from time to time.

Just a few tips and you are on your way to creating beautiful designs, and also teaching other people how to do it. No worries. Here is how to create your monkey's fist keychain in the comfort of your home.

Required Materials

- 3 ft. and 7 inches paracord (any cord or rope could be used)

- A keyring

- 1 bead

Instructions

Follow these simple steps to design your own monkeyfist keychain.

1. Make the monkey fist: First, use one end of your paracord to make a monkey's fist. Instead of paracord, we will use rope for this project. I think you can make a monkey's fist already but no worries if you can't. Here's a reminder of how to do it.

    a. Loosely cloak the rope three times around your fingers.

    b. Swaddle it thrice horizontally and vertically encircling the first three curves loosely.

c.   Use a bead or any small round objects to design the core of your monkeyfist. Here, we will use a bead.

d.   Muffle the rope three times through the vertical and horizontal gap of the wrappings to encircle the core.

e.   Stretch the rope to tighten your monkey fist knot. Just make sure you don't pull the knot's two ends.

2.   Create the hangman's noose: Design the hangman's noose and attach your keyring as soon as you finish making your monkey's fist knot. The hangman's noose will sit on the rear side of the rope. Again, create the hangman's noose if you know how to do it, and move to the next step. You can't design it? No worries. Here's how you can create the hangman's noose.

a.   Use the rope to make an S-shape and swaddle the end of the monkeyfist all over the rope's three strands.

b.   Slip the fist through the curve at that end as soon as the rope is finished and pull out the strand of rope through the other end to tighten the curve that supports the fist.

c.   Muffle the strand around the rope to make it very thick and super glue the end of the rope and the beginning of the monkey fist. But, if you choose to use a paracord for another monkey's fist keychain, melt the two ends with a lighter.

    d. Trim excess rope and attach the keyring on the noose end loop.

3. Step 3. Add finishing touches: Feel free to float your monkey fist keychain with some floating ropes. Just make sure what you are using is not as heavy as the core.

You have just designed a monkey fist keychain, congratulations.

Chapter Summary

- Celtic monkey fist is a charming ornamental knot that helps sailors throw their cables to the shore easily.

- You need a little bit of creativity and commitment to create one.

In the next chapter you will learn how to design a Celtic knot keychain.↓

Chapter Twelve:
Celtic Knot Keychain

Celtic knot designs look pleasing and attractive. Also, they are so simple that you can create them on your own with little or no supervision at all. In this chapter, I will show you how to design a few Celtic knot keychain projects. But, before then, let's quickly create a regular Celtic knot keychain now.

Required Materials

- Five 170 cm polyester cords

- Some safety pins

Instructions

Follow these simple steps to create a regular Celtic knot keychain

1. Mark the cords 10 cm apart, align, and pin them together.

2. Use the last left cord and the right cord closest to it to design a knot.

3. Use the second-to-the-last left cord and the middle cord to create another knot.

4. Repeat the process to tie yet another knot with the last right cord with the left cord closest to it.

5. Run the whole process from left to right until you tie the cords to knots, rotate the cords, and pin everything firmly to create a long chain.

6. Fold and heat the ends to bind them.

Great work. You just designed a regular Celtic knot keychain.

Celtic Knot Keychain Projects

Knotted Leather Earrings

Knotted leather earrings are nice homemade Celtic knots that you can present to your loved ones as gifts. Not only are these earrings simple, stylish, beautiful and charming, you can design them right there in your home with little or no supervision. It'll soon be the season of sending gifts to loved ones and you'll surely need to send some. Yes, creating the knotted leather earrings takes just a few minutes to complete. Beautiful, isn't it? Here's how you can create your own knotted leather earrings.

Required Materials

- Leather

- 7 inches thin leather

- A pair of scissors

- 14 pieces beadalon cord (silver-plaited c-crimp ends)

- 14 pieces 1.9 mm Beadalon c-crimp cord ends

- 60 pieces French hook earring wires (silver-plated)

- 16 pieces Beadalon ear wires (gold-plated ball and spring nickel free)

Instructions

Follow these simple steps to design your own knotted leather earrings.

1. Cut your leather to 3/8" by 4" strips. I think earrings should be small and firm on the ears of people using them, but feel free to vary the size of your strips if you love huge and long earrings.

2. Tie the leather into a simple and loose knot.

3. Bring together the tail ends of the knot and pinch them, leaving the leather's good sides to face out. Lay the c-crimp on the tail ends, hold them with your pliers, and pinch everything firmly.

4. Hold the loop of the c-crimp and clip the earring wire to its top.

5. Trim the longer strips or make the earrings dangle down a bit.

You just designed cute earrings.

Celtic Knot Pendant

People have been using this adorable knot right from the time of the Roman Empire. The Celtic knot pendant is beautiful and charming, but difficult to design. Still, with the few tips here, you will surely create your own Celtic knot pendant. Let's get started!

Required Materials

- AutoCAD

- Pendant image

- A pair of pliers

- 13/16 Craftsman socket

- Trefoil wire

- A triangle file

- Hobby file

Instructions

Follow these simple steps to design your Celtic knot pendant.

1. AutoCAD your image: First, search for your favorite pendant image online, copy, and paste it in your AutoCAD, place three arcs on it, and rotate the arcs till the image takes a circular shape. Use the trim tool to clean it up to get a simple symbol of the pendant you want to design. Check for the circle where the arcs intersect and overlap. Mark the circle.

2. Connect the wire to the circle: Connect the 14-gauge zinc-coated steel wire trefoil to the circle. Just walk in to one of the hardware stores within the neighborhood to buy it. Better still, you can place an online order for trefoil and it will be delivered to your doorstep. Form a coil with the Craftsman socket and your pair of pliers. Ensure that the size of the coil is equal to what you have on the template. Feel free to trim the coil or wind the wire to suit the lengths of the arcs. Also, mark the direction of the curves with a triangle file.

3. File the notches: Just file your notches between 45 and 90 degrees before you try to fold the pendant. Why? You need the whole thing to be neat and straight, don't you?

4. Fold the knot: Carefully bend two, out of the three arcs, together. Open the middle arc to make the arcs look like folded arms and bend in the last arc. Close the wire and open the arc with the pliers and check again to see whether

the socket is well connected for proper reshaping.

5. Weave the circle: Use the socket and pliers method to form the inner circle. Twist the parts of your trefoil a little bit to pave way for threading. Just remember that the joint lies at the back of one of the arcs. Find it.

6. Solder and polish the pendant: Quickly wrap the 16-gauge wire all over your hobby file to make a jump ring, connect the arcs, and solder the joints.

7. Remove any marks on the pendant and use a buffing wheel to polish the pendant.

You just designed a Celtic knot pendant.

Celtic Heart Knot

The Celtic heart knot is unique and adorable. It is cool for decorations or you can use it to design your jewelry. Better still, design a card with this knot, send it to someone who's special to you on Valentine or St. Patrick's Day, but be ready to be forever trapped in a pool of affection. That's the magic strength of the Celtic heart knot. Here is how to tie your own Celtic heart knot.

Required Materials

- Ropes

- Shoelaces

- Paracords

- A pair of scissors

Instructions

Follow these simple steps to tie your own Celtic heart knot.

1. Fold your cord in half to create two loops.

2. Pull the right loop to the top of the cord. Hold the right loop with your thumb and try to secure the left loop too.

3. Pass the left loop below the right one, halfway to the middle-top. Lower the left loop but pay keen attention to where the two loops intertwined. Hold the right cord, weave top, bottom, and back parts.

4. Carefully trim the Celtic knot to shape.

Celtic Knot Macramé Bracelet

The Celtic knot macramé bracelet is charming. Hundreds of years ago, the bracelet was considered as a symbol of devotion and eternal life, while its three adorable intersecting loops symbolized fire, earth, and water—the three natural elements of human existence. Still, the beauty of the Celtic knot macramé bracelet continues to amaze our generation. Yet, it is so simple that you can design it in a few minutes. How? No worries. Here is how.

Required Materials

- 72" leather cord (with 1 1/2 or 2 mm thickness)

- 4 or 6 large-hole beads

- Button for clasp

- Clipboard

- Needle and thread

- A pair of scissors

Instructions

Follow these simple steps to design your own Celtic knot macramé bracelet.

1. Tie the button clasp: Hold the center of cord, needle-thread the button, and use an overhand knot to tie the button in position.

2. Secure the button: Use your clipboard to clip your button-end firmly to the cord.

3. Start knitting: Just follow the steps here to run the knotting process.

   a. Tie the Celtic knot first and form a loop with the left cord.

b. Pass the right cord over the loop and channel it below the left-hand cord. Find the triangle space over the two cords, directly below the knot where the button is attached. Run the cord on the right through the triangle under the next cord, over the next one, under the next, and like that till you get to the last cord, and pull it through.

c. Adjust the knot to equal the two sides, and also sit the knot close to the overhand knot. Slide and place the first bead close to the knot.

d. Repeat the process to tie more Celtic knots until you have a bracelet that is one inch short of what you actually wanted to design.

4. Add final touches: Tie one more overhand knot to the bracelet, and gently pull it to tighten the Celtic knot. Create a loop by tying another overhand knot that has the same diameter with your button clasp. Run the button through the loop. Cut off the excess ends.

Now you have a finished Celtic knot macramé bracelet. Congratulations if you made it properly! Don't worry if it isn't perfect. This is a hard one! Start the process all over again and practice until you master it.

Here are a few more tips on how to design an effortless Celtic knot macramé bracelet.

1. Should you have issues laying the bracelet flat, pin the loops to a flat surface, and sit the bracelet on the spot all-night.

2. Traditional buttons have holes drilled on them and they are hard to use. But, if you want to use these buttons, just create some space between your first knot and the buttons.

3. Decide whether to use the raw or polished cording. Just know that while it is easier to work with the raw cording, you need to try polished or finished cording a few times to master it. Still, you can use silk cord, hemp, yam, or cotton twine to design your Celtic knot macramé bracelet.

4. Tie the knots near one another and do away with the beads if you want to achieve a more masculine outlook. Would you like to avoid twisting the bracelet? Knot-tie the bracelet in a reversed direction.

Chapter Summary

- Knotted leather earrings are homemade Celtic knot gifts for loved ones.

- a Celtic knot macramé bracelet is a hard project, but rewarding when you get it right.

In the next chapter you will learn a few amazing things about the trinity knot and mandalas.↓

Chapter Thirteen: Trinity Knot on a Mandala

Lots of things have been said about the Celtic trinity knot—its meanings, uses, and shape. Designing a trinity knot on a mandala is something you'll want to try since you've already designed some amazing projects. Again, mandala projects are unique and colorful, and you can vary their shapes as you like. In this chapter, I will teach you how to create your mandala and how to design a crochet mandala. Let's start with the simple mandala design.

Required Materials

- Paper of any kind, preferably art stock

- Compass

- Gold glitter pen

- White pencil

- An eraser

- White-water gel pen

Instructions

Follow these simple steps to design your own mandala.

1. Lay the paper on a surface.

2. Use the compass and white pencil to sketch a circle on it.

3. Sketch 4 evenly-spaced lines in the circle. Let the lines intersect in the circle's center to create equal angles.

4. Use your pencil to fill inner details.

5. Sketch raw highlights in the circle with the white water gel pen. Do it when you are filling the inner details.

6. Transfer the design to the slice on your mandala.

7. Creatively connect all the designs together from the right part of the circle, one after the other.

8. Use your eraser to clean up the rough outlines.

9. Add theme to the design with the golden glitter pen.

You have just designed your mandala.

How to Design a Crochet Mandala

Here is the colorful crochet mandala. It is beautiful and charming, a perfect gift for someone you really treasure. Right there in your home, you can create your own crochet mandala, and also twist the design as you want so that it is as unique as you. You want to do it straight away? No problems. Just get these materials ready and you'll be good to go.

Required Materials

- Yarn

- Crochet needle

- A pair of scissors

- Yarn or tapestry needle

- Thread (according to yarn or tapestry needle)

- Sewing machine

Instructions

Follow these simple steps to design your own crochet mandala.

2. Get mandala crochet patterns: Be inspired to create a unique crochet mandala. Download inspiring crochet patterns online. Feel free to follow the pattern or design your crochet mandala from the scratch.

3. Decide your yarn colors: Just opt for any yarn color you're okay with. If you want to vary your yarn colors, fine. Sure, that's a good way of creating a colorful effect. Also, you may opt for many colors but don't exceed three.

a. A crochet mandala with four or more colors will lose its uniqueness and you won't like the final product. Still, consider using bright colors to make your mandala vibrant and attractive. Pastels, neutral shades, and other subdued colors are equally good for the project.

b. Yarn colors to alternate to get bright and colorful mandalas are red, yellow, orange, pink, purple, blue, and green. But, if a subdued mandala is your favorite, use aqua, light-pink, brown, light-yellow, or light-blue yarn.

4. Single out your decorative stitches: Use a simple decorative stitch to design your crochet mandala. And, if you like, you can combine the two to create a striking effect. Single or double crochet are the simple stitches options you can bank on. Also, depending on what you want, choose any of these decorative stitches—heart, rosebud, moss, shell, and camel stitches. Still, you can give your crochet mandala some intricate designs. How? Choose some decorative stitches and design them back and forth on your mandala.

5. Step 4. Create the circles: Feel free to make your circles wide or narrow. Just remember that the circles will determine the size of your crochet mandala. Again, your circles depend on

how often you vary the yarn color. Still, after 2 rounds of narrow circles, change the yarn. For wider circles, wait till you have 4 rounds.

   a. Also, you may create your favorite pattern for this, just to strike a beautiful balance. To strike this beautiful balance, a 4-round circle of yellow could follow a 2-round circle of blue before you add another 2-round circle of red, but strive to use the pattern that works best for you. Use a slipknot to crochet a ring on the rounds of the mandala and wrap the yarn twice all over your index and middle fingers.

6. Step 5. Double-stitch the crochet: Create 3 crochet chains and wrap them all over the ring eleven times to form a double crochet stitch. Next, double-crochet each circle for eleven times until you attain 12 stitches in the first round. Still, you may decide to run a single crochet all through the first round to make the round a little bit narrow.

   a. Gradually, as you expand the circle, feel free to add more stitches but pay keen attention to the pattern you adopted for your crochet mandala. Still, don't let the stitches you are starting with exceed 12 if you don't want to end up with ruffled circles.

7. Slip stitch your circles: Don't leave any circle open when you are designing your crochet

mandala. Slip stitch the opening of each crochet chain once you hit the end of a round. But make sure you attach the hook of the crotchet before the opening of the chain is stitched. Next, cover the stitch with yarn and run it through.

8. Double-crochet the stitch: Use 2 double crochet stitches for each round. But, if you are working with single stitches, just double them. Sustain the stitches through the rounds. Should you desire a narrower round, use a single crochet all through this stage.

9. Switch colors and start another round: Cut the previous yarn 15 cm away from the last stitch, join the new yarn to its base, and align it with the previous stitch. Just use your simple decorative stitch to design the new round.

    a. It all depends on what you want. Your mandala could be large or small. But, if you are trying to replicate the mandala pattern, you'll need to stick to its size. Again, always consider the suitability of your design for what you want to use the mandala for. Opt for smaller mandalas if you're designing them for coasters while larger ones are great for decorative tablecloths and potholders. Just make sure you create rounds that could support the size of your crochet mandala.

10. Weave the end of the yarn: Weave the tail of the round you just completed. Use s different thread colors to stitch the yarn. A tapestry or yarn needle can be used to do the stitching. So, carefully and stylishly sew the tail of the yarn with the rows of stitches you already designed. Adopt the technique you used to weave the end of your yarn in the previous round. Run the yarn through the previous stitch and tie it to firmly hold or secure your crochet mandala. Still, make sure you weave it with your tapestry or yarn needle.

You just designed your own crochet mandala.

Pay keen attention to the weight of your yarn to know the right crochet hook to use for the design. For example, you'll need a 5.5 mm hook for a medium-weighted yarn. Anything short of this could mess up the whole project. But, if you're working with a bulky yarn, make sure the size of your crochet hook is at least 9 mm. How can I know what size of crochet hook I need? Check the label of the yarn.

Use mechanical pencils to trace your mandala patterns. With the fine tip of the pencil, you can easily create delicate and detailed drawings. Opt for pentel clic erasers since they are pen lookalikes and you can easily use these erasers to clean small areas. Also, the erasers are very effective on pencil marks.

Chapter Summary

- Mandala projects are unique, colorful, and you can vary their shapes as you want.

- You can obtain mandala patterns on the internet, or you can design your own.

In the next chapter you will learn how to design khala patterns with color enhancement.↓

Chapter Fourteen: Khala Pattern with Color Enhancement

The khala pattern looks like a triangle. It is actually one of several patterns used in designing Celtic knots. Khala patterns can enhance the aesthetics and make your Celtic knots beautiful and appealing. Yet, beginners and intermediate quilters often say that khala patterns are hard to draw. Sure, crafting nice khala patterns requires a bunch of creativity and dedication. With creativity, you can design the perfect khala pattern for the Celtic project you want to create, while dedication keeps you focused all through the process. No worries. In this chapter, I will teach you how to use colored pencils to draw your own khala pattern.

Required Materials

- Grainy paper

- Water colors

- Water dropper

- Pencil colors

- Synthetic brushes

- Cotton buds

Instructions

Follow these simple steps to draw your khala pattern.

1. Carefully use your brush to sprinkle some drops of water on the grainy paper.

2. Use the dropper to apply purple and blue colors around the edges of your paper. Use your favorite colors if you don't like the ones suggested here.

3. Spread the colors all over the paper to form a few triangles. Also, fill the triangles with matching colors.

4. Use your cotton boards to absorb excess water from the grainy paper so that the colors can sit well on the paper.

5. Draw lines on the paper with your white pencil color. The lines should start from the edges of your paper to the center of the paper.

6. Sketch the shape of the pattern on your paper. Use the black pen to do the drawing and also fill empty space.

7. Shade the pattern with your water and pencil colors. Also, highlight the design with your white charcoal pencil. Remember that drawings sketched with the white charcoal

pencil cannot be erased. So, carefully run this stage if you want to perfect it.

8. Fill deep details of the pattern with the water gel pen. Also, use the water pencils to saturate and balance the pattern's embellishments.

9. Use your black charcoal pencil to adorn the pattern with shadows to make it look like a 3D design.

Congratulations, you just designed your beautiful colored khala pattern. The design can be used in many ways. You could turn it to a stencil or simply use it as a decor. It all depends on what you want to do with it.

How to Organize or Save Your Khala Patterns

Sure, the internet is saturated with lots of khala patterns you can use to design adorable Celtic projects. But, most of the time, finding the perfect pattern can be challenging. Yes, sites like Google and Pinterest have both good and bad patterns. The thing is, you'll have to first sort out the bad ones before you can get the right khala patterns for your Celtic projects, which is a waste of time. Find a way to organize and save downloaded khala patterns or the ones you designed from the scratch. Here, I'll be showing you three different ways you could organize and save your khala patterns.

Journals, Books, and Sketchbooks

Simply draw your khala patterns in a blank journal or sketchbook so that you can easily track them. Depending on your preference, you can opt for graph papers, dot-grid journals, or sketchbooks with blank pages. Just make sure that you are using the journals, books, or sketchbooks for khala patterns alone, since that will save you the stress of finding the right patterns for your imminent Celtic projects.

Feel free to create your khala patterns on Post-It-Notes. Just move the patterns to your journal or sketchbook. How? Copy it from where you drew the pattern and paste it in the journal or sketchbook. It is that simple! Sue Jacobs, the first person to share the idea of the Post-It-Notes, affirmed that the Post-It-Notes option is a unique way one can arrange and save one's khala patterns on journals and sketchbooks.

Again, rather than using blank sketchbooks, sketch your khala patterns in pre-printed notebooks with boxes that could be filled with lovely colors. Here are some of these pre-printed notebooks.

- Storyboard notebooks: These notebooks come with printed empty boxes for sketching scenes when a writer prepares a script. Just as writers use the notebooks for scripting purposes, Celtic art designers can use storyboard notebooks to arrange and save their khala patterns in journals and sketchbooks.

- Blank comic book: This is a series of pre-printed comic book panels that can accommodate your khala patterns. Just sketch your khala patterns into the notebook's empty panels, copy the patterns, and paste them into your journals and sketchbooks.

Binders and Plastic Sheets

Downloaded khala patterns can be saved in a binder. It is easy, safe, and quick. So, whether it is a whole sheet of khala patterns or just a few simple khala designs, save them in your binder. When there's a Celtic knot to design, simply open your binder, choose your favorite pattern, and get started with the design.

Feel free to save your khala patterns in plastic card protectors. Again, these protectors are durable and better than regular hole-punched notebooks. Here are the available options for plastic card protectors.

- Full sheet protectors: These protectors are perfect for full-sheet khala patterns.

- Baseball card protectors: These protectors come with index and artist trading cards, and they can be used to design amazing khala patterns. Downloaded khala patterns can be saved on the index or artist trading cards until you need them to create your colorful Celtic patterns.

Ring-Bound Flashcards

There are flash cards and flip cards that you can use to save your khala patterns. It is very easy to add, rearrange, or remove the khala patterns saved on these cards. And, for reference purposes especially when you're sketching your khala patterns, feel free to remove the flash cards from the ring. Visit Amazon or Jetpens to get these flashcards to store your khala patterns.

Chapter Summary

- Khala patterns are used for designing Celtic knots because they are beautiful and appealing.

- You need to be creative to design a perfect khala pattern.